M000250001

Wonderful 1-BLOCK QUILTING

Quick & Easy Techniques for Small Projects to Full-Size Quilts

Choly Knight

DESIGN ORIGINALS
an Imprint of Fox Chapel Publishing
www.d-originals.com

ACQUISITION EDITOR: Peg Couch
COPY EDITOR: Laura Taylor
COVER AND LAYOUT DESIGNER: Ashley Millhouse
EDITOR: Katie Weeber
PROJECT PHOTOGRAPHY: Scott Kriner
STEP-BY-STEP PHOTOGRAPHY: Matthew McClure

ISBN 978-1-4972-0008-1

Library of Congress Cataloging-in-Publication Data

Knight, Choly.
  Wonderful one-block quilting / Choly Knight.
    pages cm
  Includes index.
  ISBN 978-1-4972-0008-1
  1. Patchwork--Patterns. 2. Quilting--Patterns. I. Title.
  TT835.K5645 2015
  746.46--dc23
              2015018259

COPY PERMISSION: The written instructions, photographs, designs, patterns, and projects in this publication are intended for the personal use of the reader and may be reproduced for that purpose only. Any other use, especially commercial use, is forbidden under law without the written permission of the copyright holder. Every effort has been made to ensure that all information in this book is accurate. However, due to differing conditions, tools, and individual skills, neither the author nor publisher can be responsible for any injuries, losses, or other damages which may result from the use of the information in this book.
INFORMATION: All rights reserved. All images in this book have been reproduced with the knowledge and prior consent of the artists concerned and no responsibility is accepted by producer, publisher, or printer for any infringement of copyright or otherwise, arising from the contents of this publication. Every effort has been made to ensure that credits accurately comply with information supplied.
WARNING: Due to the components used in this craft, children under 8 years of age should not have access to materials or supplies without adult supervision. Under rare circumstances components of products could cause serious or fatal injury. Please read all safety warnings for the products being used. Neither New Design Originals, the product manufacturer, or the supplier is responsible.
NOTE: The use of products and trademark names is for informational purposes only, with no intention of infringement upon those trademarks.

© 2015 by Choly Knight and New Design Originals Corporation, *www.d-originals.com*, an imprint of Fox Chapel Publishing, 800-457-9112, 1970 Broad Street, East Petersburg, PA 17520.

Printed in Singapore
First printing

About the Author

Choly Knight is from Orlando, Florida, and is the author of *Sew Kawaii!, Sew Baby, Sewing Stylish Handbags & Totes, Sew Me! Sewing Basics, Sew Me! Sewing Home Décor, Sew Me! Sew and Go, Quilting Simplified, Bling It Up!, Awesome Duct Tape Projects, Craft Projects for Minecraft® and Pixel Art Fans,* and *Pixel Craft with Perler Beads.* She has been crafting for as long as she can remember, and has drawn, painted, sculpted, and stitched everything in sight. She began sewing clothing in 1997 and has yet to put her sewing machine away. After studying studio art and earning a BA in English, she now enjoys trying to find numerous different ways to combine her passions for writing, fine art, and craft art. She created all of the designs, projects, and patterns that appear in this book. She focuses on handcrafted clothing, accessories, and other creations inspired by Japanese art, anime, and style, and specializes in cosplay (costume play) hats and hoodies. You can find out more about her and her work on her website: *www.cholyknight.com.*

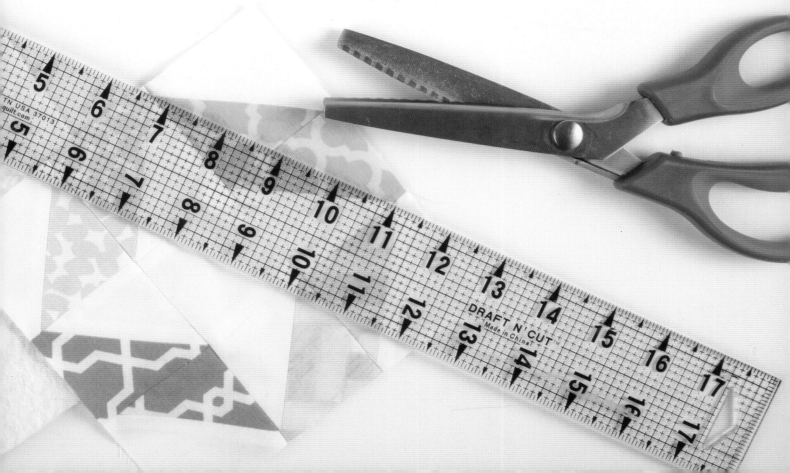

Introduction

My first quilt was made primarily out of necessity, but I never imagined how addicted I would become. I started sewing by making my own clothes and accessories, and any sewer will tell you how quick and easy it is to amass a huge stash of fabric scraps after only a few projects. I had squirreled away an unmanageable trove of fabric beneath my bed, and I tried every trick up my sleeve to get rid of it: gift purses for friends, matching hats for all of my outfits, and every other trinket you can imagine.

But I was ignoring the elephant in the room—quilts. I learned from sewing books that quilts are the quintessential scrap-busting project; used from the very onset of sewing history. But I was convinced that quilting was way beyond my ability—it seemed like an art only practiced by skilled masters who could sew precise ¼" (0.5cm) seams without even looking and used an arsenal of templates, rulers, and guides for even the most basic projects. I felt I couldn't even think about quilting until I was a seasoned veteran sewer. Meanwhile my closets were quickly filling with scraps and I was drowning in fabric.

Before it was too late, I decided I had to sew myself out of the fabric pile I had created. I didn't have many of the fancy templates and tools that dedicated quilters do, but I studied to find shortcuts, tricks, and techniques that allowed me to make the quilt I wanted without so many hard and fast rules.

Even though my first quilt was unusual to say the least—made from an eclectic mix of satins, denim, and cotton with more than a handful of wonky seams and frayed edges—I was surprised by how much I loved the process. Watching a tiny swatch of fabric slowly grow into a massive quilt top through all that piecing was breathtaking to me. Not to mention I loved how quilting turned a random pile of fabric into an intricate collage with so much depth and texture. I was immediately hooked.

I hope that when you start to see the quilting possibilities ahead of you, you will be hooked too. Taking the plunge into quilting can be intimidating, which is why I'll focus here on small one-block projects. These projects will introduce you to the quilting process on a small scale, so there's no need to feel overwhelmed. I'll teach you everything I know about making the process as easy as possible. You'll find uncommon and underrated techniques that make quilting approachable and foolproof. And each new technique is followed by a manageable project to test your skills, so you can practice before taking on a large bed quilt. And you'll have a beautiful patchwork project to boot! You'll find that each project includes fabric requirements and cutting plans for five different quilt sizes. These are ready and waiting for you once you've had the chance to practice and gain confidence with the smaller projects.

Creating a quilted project will likely be a challenging endeavor your first time, but I think you'll find it's worth it for the immense payoff you receive. Not only will your project be a unique, handmade item that will last for years, but it will also serve as a time capsule. Quilts and quilted projects are a beautiful way of showcasing a collection of favorite fabrics and motifs that you fell in love with at a particular time in your life.

So whether you're ready to try patchwork for the first time or are completely comfortable with quilting and need some quick weekend projects, I'm sure you'll find something new to learn from this book!

Happy quilting!

32

58

88

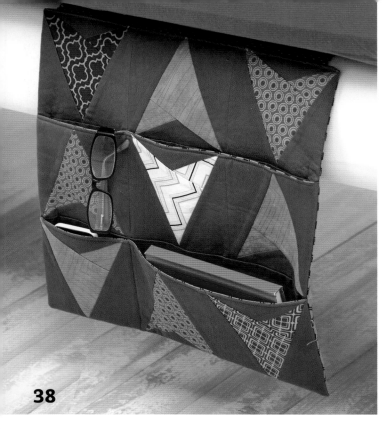

38

48

78

68

98

Getting Started

If you've never quilted before, this is the place to start! Preparing to quilt might seem like a daunting task, but in truth, you don't need a whole lot to get started. This book describes the most basic of tools and techniques that will open a wealth of possibilities, and you won't get bogged down with extra gadgets and rules you don't need to know just yet. Take note of this section during your next shopping trip so you'll know exactly what to look for!

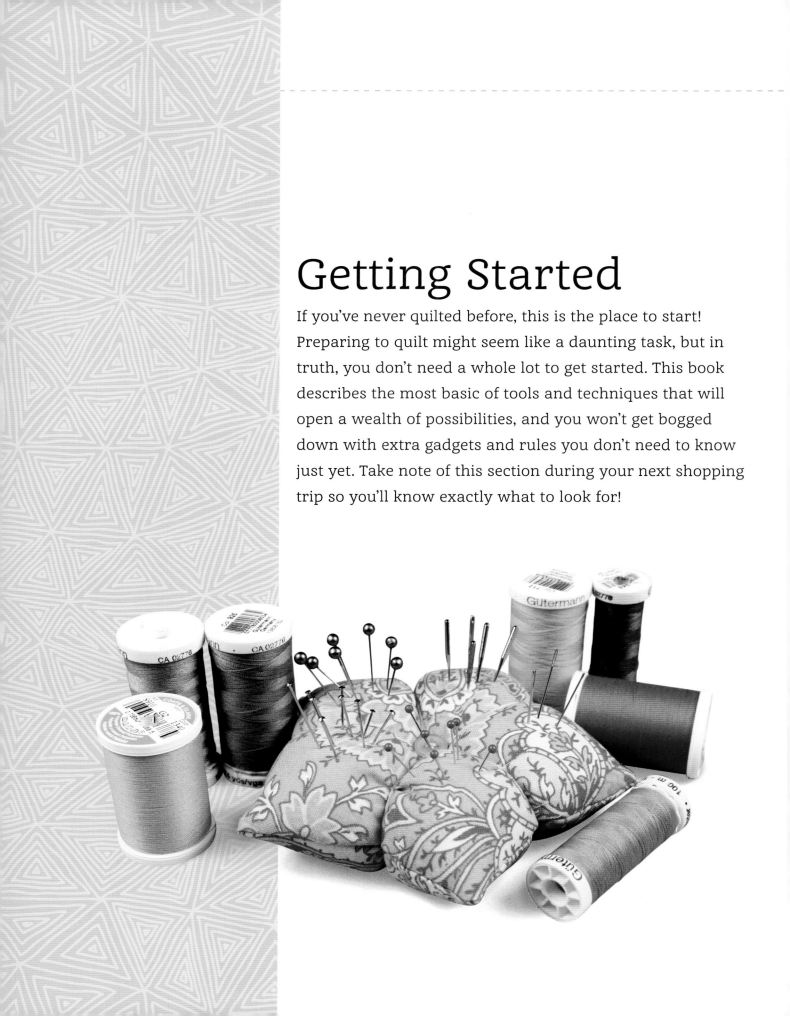

THE HARDWARE: Essential Quilting Tools

The first time you venture into the quilting tools section of your local fabric store, you might be surprised to find that there's a quilting tool for practically every style of quilt out there. The truth is that you only need a few select tools to get the ball rolling. (You can treat yourself to the fancy gadgets later!) These are the most basic quilting tools to get you started and ones you'll use for the lifetime of your quilting pursuit, so treat them well and look forward to all the fun you'll get to have with them!

Sewing machine: If you're looking into buying a new machine for quilting, know that a reliable mechanical machine with only a straight stitch and a zigzag stitch can make just about any kind of quilt. So, yes, you can use your regular sewing machine if you already have one. But if you're in the market to buy a machine and a fancy model has caught your eye, consider the features you want before pulling out your wallet. These are all options that can make quilting easier, but are not required. And many of these features are available on sewing machines not designed for quilting, so again, a regular mechanical machine will serve you just fine to get started.

TIP

If you're finding the shopping process too overwhelming, consider shopping at a quilting store instead of a fabric shop. You won't get bogged down by non-quilting items, and the employees there can help you every step of the way!

• • • • • • • • • • • • • • •

- **Adjustable feed dogs:** Just about every quilting machine will come with this feature, but not all general sewing machines will. In order to do free-motion quilting (page 76), you'll need to drop the feed dogs in your machine so that you're free to move the quilt around without the machine trying to move it for you.

- **Throat space:** Most quilting sewing machines have a larger area between the needle and side panel than general machines. This gives you more room to work with your quilt while machine quilting. If you plan to do your own machine quilting (see page 74) in the future, you should definitely look for this option.

- **Extension table:** The second-most-common feature in quilting sewing machines is an extension table. These typically snap onto your machine to give you a large flat space to the left of the machine on which to rest your quilt while you piece or machine quilt. This makes machine quilting a bit easier, but not nearly as much as extra throat space does.

Quilting sewing machine. These machines will look much the same as typical sewing machines, but with some added features to make quilting a bit easier. The extended table is usually a dead giveaway. Don't feel like you have to run out and buy one of these to make a quilt—your regular home sewing machine is definitely enough to get you started.

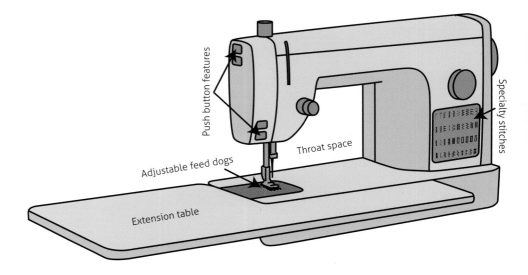

Push button features

Specialty stitches

Throat space

Adjustable feed dogs

Extension table

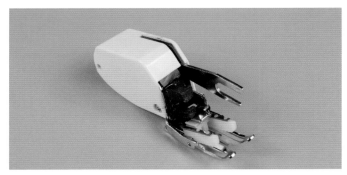

Walking foot. Also called an even-feed foot, this foot takes an extra bit of installation, but it's worth the effort. It simulates a second set of feed dogs going above the fabric, ensuring that all layers of your quilt run through the machine at the same rate.

Piecing foot (optional). A piecing foot (also called a patchwork foot or ¼" foot), has a distinctive ridge that extends on the side of the foot. You can butt your seams against this while you sew for better accuracy.

Darning foot (optional). Also called an embroidery foot. The open needle area and spring-powered pressure allow you to move your project freehand while you sew. It offers just enough pressure to hold on to your work without giving any resistance.

- **Walking foot:** There are lots of specialty feet you can purchase for your machine, but this is the only one you'll really need to do your own quilting. Also called an even-feed foot, this machine foot enables you to machine quilt your quilt layers without worry of puckers or wrinkles caused by one layer of the quilt feeding through the machine at a different rate than the others. Some quilting sewing machines have this built in, but you can just as easily purchase this foot separately.

- **Piecing foot:** Specialty sewing machines often come with extra sewing machine feet that perform interesting functions. One of these is a piecing foot. It has a ridge that extends precisely ¼" (6mm) out from your needle position, resulting in a ¼" (6mm) seam every time you sew with it. It's not a necessity (see page 28 for alternatives), but it really makes piecing foolproof. Note that you can purchase this foot separately—it doesn't have to come bundled with a new machine.

- **Darning foot:** Also called an embroidery foot, this presser foot enables you to do free-motion quilting. In conjunction with lowering your feed dogs, this foot allows you to quilt your project by moving the quilt freehand beneath the needle without the machine pulling the fabric through. This means you can go in any direction and, with some practice, create lots of intricate designs.

- **Specialty stitches:** Decorative stitches are a very common feature of high-end machines, often reaching hundreds of options with some models. I personally prefer large, less dainty forms of embellishment. If considering this option, you should think about your desired finished result before you become infatuated with the surplus of stitches available on specialty machines. Do most of your quilt project plans involve intricate decorative stitches, or are you working toward a clean and simple look? Tiny embellishing stitches are fun for some creations, but I don't think you'll end up using them in most quilting projects.

- **Push-button features:** Do mundane tasks like lowering your presser foot, lowering or raising your needle, cutting threads, or threading your needle slow you down? If these little chores really irritate you, you'll be happy to know many high-end quilting machines have push button features to take care of them for you. It raises the price tag, but if that convenience saves you loads of frustration, you might consider it!

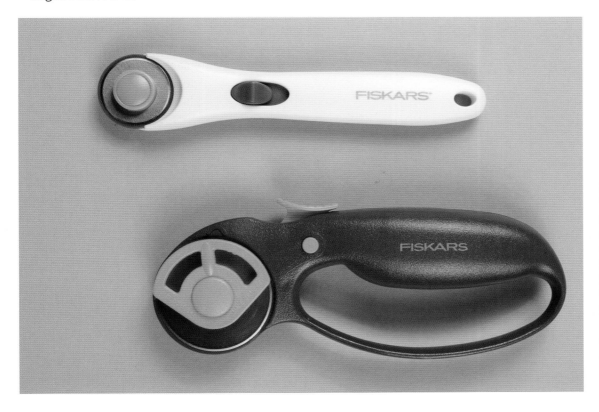

Rotary cutters. This tool is like an extremely sharp pizza cutter for fabric. Used in conjunction with a cutting mat and ruler, it ensures extremely consistent and accurate straight cuts.

Rotary cutter: As a quilter, you'll mostly be doing straight-line fabric cutting. While regular sewing shears can accomplish this just fine, the most efficient way to make straight cuts is with a rotary cutter. It works just like a pizza cutter, but is far sharper for cutting fabric. For best results, you'll need to use it in conjunction with a ruler and cutting mat. For safety, be sure to use the safety latch and replace the blade as soon as it becomes dull (usually after three quilts or so). Rotary cutters come as small as 18mm in diameter and as large as 60mm; smaller sizes work nicely for intricate curved cuts, while larger sizes are best for simple straight cuts. To get started, try a 45mm or 60mm size (depending on which feels more comfortable in your hand) and consider getting more sizes as your skills progress. See page 24 to learn how to use this tool properly.

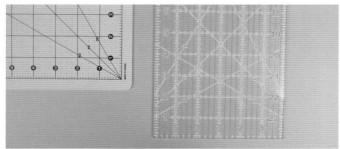

Ruler and cutting mat. A quilting ruler (at right) allows you to accurately measure and cut rectangles and various angles, while a cutting mat (at left) absorbs the nicks from your cutting blade. You will frequently work with them together.

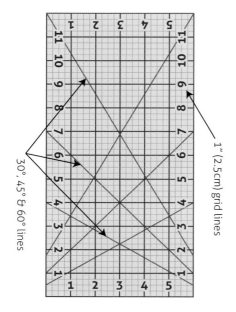

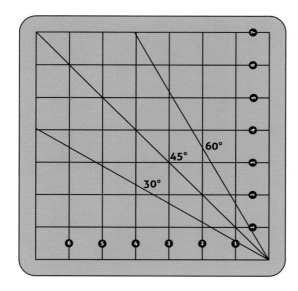

Quilting ruler: The word *ruler* might cause you to visualize the simple wooden one from elementary school, but quilting rulers are an entirely different animal. They're square or rectangular in shape, transparent, and have a grid printed over the entire surface, allowing you to measure squares and strips in a flash. You'll use this as a guide, running your rotary cutter against it to churn out quilting pieces in no time at all. (Note that rulers come marked with either inches or metric measurements, but you should never mix them on the same project.) A simple 12" x 6" (30 x 15cm) ruler is usually enough to get started, but you might consider getting a 24" (60cm)-long ruler (along with some other smaller rulers for detail work) as you build your repertoire. Be sure to look for rulers with ¼" (6mm) grid lines; a 30-, 45-, and 60-degree line is an added plus.

Cutting mat: This last crucial part of your cutting trio should have a grid printed on it, just like your quilting ruler. (Some even come with inches on one side and metrics on the other.) The mat is made out of a material that can stand up to the abuse caused by your ultra-sharp rotary cutter blade. When cutting, you'll rest your fabric and ruler on this mat; it absorbs all the cutting damage so your table doesn't have to! You can also use the grid guides in tandem with your quilting ruler to get the most accurate measurements. Large mats (such as 24" x 36" [61 x 92cm]) are easier to work on, but you won't want a mat that's larger than your worktable. If it's a better fit, a smaller 18" x 24" (45 x 60cm) mat will work just as well.

Sewing shears: While most of your fabric cutting will be done with a rotary cutter, sewing shears are still a staple of the quilting workspace, as you'll need them for cutting curved shapes in fabric. Even a cheap pair of sewing shears will cut better than regular utility scissors, especially if you treat them right and only use them on fabric. Paper, thread, and other materials can quickly dull the edge of a pair of shears.

Crafting scissors: For all of your non-fabric cutting needs, be they templates, paper patterns, or thread, a simple pair of comfortable crafting scissors will do the trick.

Iron & ironing board: Pressing your sewn seams as you work is crucial to achieving good quilting results. A basic iron and ironing board work just fine, but make sure both items are clean and in good working order. Spritzing clean water from a spray bottle onto your fabric just before pressing can also help steam your seams flat.

Sewing machine needles: Universal sewing needles are okay to use for a quick project, but long-term piecing will go better with quilting needles in the $70/10$–$80/12$ range. Machine quilting will require some heavier needles—ranging up to $90/14$ or more if you find needle breakage to be a problem. Also consider Microtex machine needles. These have a super thin, acute point, which produces more accurate stitches for techniques like topstitching. Be sure to replace your needle when it starts to get dull—after every quilt or so.

Sewing pins: These temporarily hold your fabric pieces together while you're in the process of sewing them. Long, sharp pins work best for quilting, especially ones with flat heads that lie flush against the fabric while you sew or iron.

Basting glue: As an alternative to sewing pins, basting glue works to temporarily hold your fabric together while you sew. It's more precise than pins, less cumbersome, and washes out with water. It isn't reusable like sewing pins, though, so it's best saved for cases when it's especially helpful, such as for foundation piecing and some appliqué.

Seam ripper: Just like with any other kind of project, mistakes can happen, and this little tool will take care of ripping out stitches without damaging your fabric. Don't be afraid to use it, as going back and fixing a little error is better than starting all over.

Fabric marker: It might not seem like it, but the ability to make little marks on your fabric can do wonders to help with assembly. You can use a fabric marker where pins fall short to match up areas that need to be sewn precisely. A dark water- or air-soluble marker works best on light fabrics, while a light pencil or tailor's chalk works nicely on dark fabrics.

Organization: Quilting can involve working with lots of little pieces at one time, so if you're the type who prefers to keep things tidy, consider investing in some organizing supplies, such as plastic bags, boxes, and sticky notes for your stacks of fabric pieces. You can label and bundle fabric bits while they're not in use, and you'll be sure they're ready for you the next time you sit down to sew.

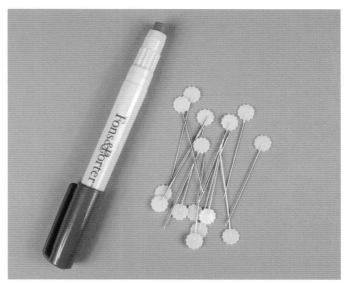

Pins and glue. Options for holding your fabric together while you sew include pins and basting glue. While pins with round heads will work, those with flat heads are most convenient because they lie flat against your fabric while you work. Basting glue is a nice alternative for hard-to-reach areas.

THE QUILTER'S TOOLKIT

The tool lists in this book mention a quilter's toolkit. These basic supplies are required for every project. Refer to this list to see what you need.

- Sewing machine
- Rotary cutter
- Quilting ruler
- Cutting mat
- Sewing shears
- Crafting scissors
- Iron & ironing board
- Sewing machine needles
- Sewing pins
- Seam ripper
- Fabric marker/pencil
- Basting glue
- Organizational tools: plastic bags, sticky notes, etc.

THE SOFTWARE: Quilting Materials

Once you have all the necessary tools, the second half of your shopping adventure involves gathering your quilting materials. This is all the soft stuff you'll use in conjunction with your handy new tools. Items like fabric and batting will reflect your own personal style, as you get to select the color, texture, and overall feel. I'll provide some tips to help you make your choices so you wind up happy with your purchases.

Quilting cotton. 100% quilting cotton, with its dense weave and bright patterns, is perfectly suited for making quilts that will last for generations. You'll find it in prints of different sizes and colors, as well as solids.

FABRIC

Choosing fabric for your quilt is a whole process unto itself; in fact, entire books have been written on the subject. It's akin to picking the paint colors for an entire painting, so it can seem complicated. But there are tricks and shortcuts you can use to avoid becoming overwhelmed. For now, I say pick fabrics that will net you the most fun, and save some of the more complicated elements of fabric selection for when you're a seasoned quilter!

The old standbys

After quilting cotton, the rest of the fabrics here are virtually interchangeable. They will have their own quirks and characteristics, but for the most part will behave like quilting cotton, just with less durability over time.

100% quilting cotton: Quilting cotton, sometimes called calico or broadcloth, is the go-to fabric for quilting because of its dense weave of fibers. It stands up to all of the needle piercing, plus the ironing and washing quilts usually endure for many years—and it will get softer over time to boot. It comes in a wealth of colors and patterns and is usually stiff and sturdy thanks to the dense weave and the layers of ink used to make those cheerful designs. When you visit a dedicated quilting shop, you will likely find only 100% quilting cotton.

QUILT BACKING

The back of your quilt (see page 25 for the anatomy of a quilt) should typically be made from quilting cotton or a sturdy material similar to the front of your quilt. If you're making a particularly large quilt, you might have to piece the quilt back (see page 64), but keep an eye out for extra-wide quilt backing fabric while shopping. It's typically available in broadcloth and flannel. The colors and designs are often limited, but you never know when one might match your design perfectly.

Linen. Though prone to unraveling, linen has a distinctive old-world charm that lends itself well to small patchwork projects.

Flannel. A much softer and warmer alternative to quilting cotton, flannel isn't quite as hard-wearing, but it's still just as easy to work with.

Flannel: Like a plushy cousin of quilting cotton, flannel is just as stable, but with some added fuzziness and loft. It does tend to pill and unravels a little more easily than quilting cotton, but it's wonderfully cozy, and the colors available are particularly suitable for babies and kids.

Linen: One hundred percent linen and linen cotton blends have a wonderful homey, earthy quality that looks beautiful in home décor projects. Working with linen requires extra care, however, because the threads tend to unravel very easily.

Unconventional fabrics

Some quilters get started because they dream of creating a quilt from old clothes—perhaps favorite old t-shirts or items left to them by a beloved family member. Experts say that beginners should steer clear of any fabric other than quilting cotton, but this book is about modern quilting, which means bending the rules! It's possible to make patchwork pieces from other fabrics—you'll just have to change your technique a bit. Methods like increasing your seam allowance, foundation piecing (page 36), tying your quilt (page 67), or simply choosing a pattern with larger patchwork pieces will increase your chances of success. Unconventional quilting fabrics will throw you some curveballs now and again, so all in all it's best to have lots of foolproof techniques at your disposal when using them.

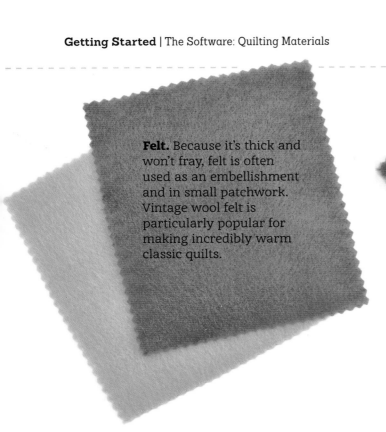

Felt. Because it's thick and won't fray, felt is often used as an embellishment and in small patchwork. Vintage wool felt is particularly popular for making incredibly warm classic quilts.

Fleece, corduroy, and velvet. Fleece is extremely soft and plush and best suited for quilts with large patchwork. Corduroy is a winning combination of sturdy and soft. It's best suited for large patchwork or patchwork where accuracy isn't an issue. Velvet is a real luxury, so it must be handled carefully to tame its tricky qualities. Foundation piecing is one good way of lending it some stability.

Felt: Felt is kind of in a class all its own; it's made from pressed wool fibers and doesn't fray like typical quilting fabrics. This makes it perfect for embellishments like appliqué, but it's also suitable for any patchwork with large pieces. Try to steer clear of acrylic or polyester felts, as they don't behave nearly as well as their all-natural wool counterpart.

Corduroy: Corduroy blends the softness of flannel with the sophistication of linen. Thin wale varieties are perfect for quilting, as they aren't too thick and can handle lots of patchwork. Medium wale varieties also work well, but will require larger seam allowances and patchwork sizes.

Fleece: This plush fabric might not seem like a good fit for quilts, but in some cases it works really well! For instance, fleece can often be used as a replacement for quilt batting or for patchwork projects with large pieces. Wearable items and baby items look especially nice with the color choices available.

Velvet: Sort of like the luxurious cousin of corduroy, velvet is extremely soft, but requires some special care to sew. It behaves better with large seam allowances and patchwork pieces. Foundation piecing (page 36) helps the most when working with velvet, because the fabric tends to shift while you sew it. Ironing may

also be tricky; you can iron velvet carefully by placing it face down on a towel and using a press cloth. Or simply throw caution to the wind and use the iron directly on the fabric (set to a low temperature); you'll just end up with crushed velvet instead—not a bad payoff! For more inspiration, do some research on Victorian crazy quilts, where you'll often encounter velvet and satin fabrics.

Satin: While probably the most finicky of the unconventional fabrics, satin can be tamed using foundation piecing (page 36) and large seam allowances. Brocades tend to be sturdier than other satins, but they all fray quite a bit and have a delicate weave. Don't go too heavy on the quilting (quilt tying is a better option), because satin can't stand up to hard wear. Satins also work well as accents, used in conjunction with more stable fabrics like corduroy or quilting cotton.

What to avoid

Some fabrics are more trouble than they are worth when it comes to quilting. These include thin, stretchy fabrics like jersey or Lycra; heavy, stiff fabrics like canvas; and anything heavily ornamented or embroidered like jacquard.

HOW QUILTING COTTONS ARE SOLD

You will most commonly find fabrics in the store rolled up on bolts. The fabric is then cut from the bolt in the yardage you need (usually in increments of ⅛ yd. [10cm]) by your friendly fabric shop employee. The fabric on the bolt can range from 42"–44" (105-112cm) wide and 8–10 yd. (8–10m) long. The materials list for your selected pattern will tell you how many yards to buy. But that's not the only way quilting fabrics are sold.

Fat quarters: The second most common fabric cut seen in fabric stores is the fat quarter. These are often sold neatly wrapped and folded, allowing you to grab a large variety without a trip to the cutting counter. Fat quarters are available in both the metric and the English measurement system (the one that uses inches and yards and is most common in the United States), but their dimensions will be different.

In the English system, a regular ¼ yard (roughly 23cm) cut of fabric measures 9" x 42" (about 23 x 106.5cm), but a fat quarter is cut from the corner of 1 yard (91.5cm) of fabric, creating a piece that's 18" x 21" (about 45.5 x 53.5cm). Metric fat quarters are also cut from the corner of the fabric, but in this case from 1 meter of cloth, so they measure 50 x 55cm (roughly 19½" x 21½").

Fat quarters allow you to cut wider squares and other shapes from the fabric than a narrower, regular quarter of a yard (or quarter of a meter) strip would allow.

Fat eighths: Not as common as fat quarters, fat eighths are also cut along the width of the fabric, resulting in a wider 9" x 21" (23 x 53.5cm) square. (They measure 50 x 27cm in the metric system.)

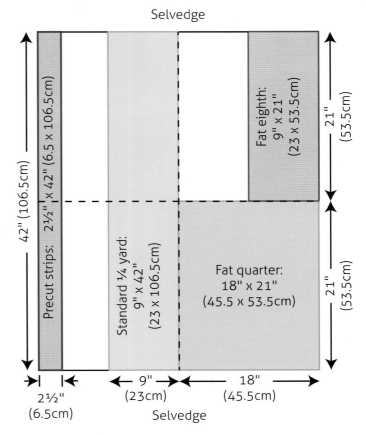

Precut squares: Also known as charm squares or layer cakes, precut squares are bundles of fabric squares ranging from 5" x 5" (12.5 x 12.5cm) to 10" x 10" (25.5 x 25.5cm). These are perfect if you want to make a quilt with a small repeating block that varies in color throughout.

Precut strips: Sometimes known as jelly rolls or honey buns, these are strips that range from 1"–3" (2.5–7.5cm) by the width of the fabric from which they were cut. They're perfect for quilts with lots of stripes or tiny squares.

Thread. Because quilts include so many colors at once, it's much simpler to pick out a high-quality thread in a neutral color that blends nicely with all your fabrics. Pick a bright color if your quilt is monochromatic.

THREAD

A little spool of thread might seem humble, but between piecing and quilting, your project is going to have several spools of thread holding it together by the time you finish. So be sure to get the best quality thread you can afford.

Polyester: Polyester thread is considered a universal thread that's great for all sewing projects, so there's no need to hesitate about using this synthetic material.

Cotton: Cotton thread is a great choice for purists who prefer to make quilts of heirloom quality. Steer clear of hand-quilting thread for piecing, as this thread has a waxy coating that won't play well with your machine.

After you've selected the type of thread you'd like to use, the question of color is really quite easy. Simply choose a neutral color that blends in nicely with all of your fabrics and is unlikely to stand out amidst your patchwork. Shades of gray work well with cool color schemes, while beige blends in nicely with warm color schemes (see page 20 for more about color schemes).

BATTING

Batting is the fluffy layer placed between the quilt top and quilt bottom. It's usually sold in precut packages that correspond to common quilt and quilt project sizes. It's also sold by the yard in widths that reach up to 120" (305cm). Double-check the measurements of your finished project so you can select batting that fits your creation perfectly. See page 66 for more information about assembling a quilt.

Cotton: Cotton batting is a dense, natural batting that's much thinner than polyester and easy to quilt through. It usually shrinks in the wash. In a finished quilt, this shrinkage typically produces a pleasant crinkly effect that most quilters love.

Fusible fleece interfacing: While technically more interfacing than batting, fusible fleece is an iron-on batting that adds stability to the fabric you adhere it to, while also adding a bit of loft. It's great for small quilting projects because you don't have to worry about basting. It also works for any other project that benefits from stability without becoming too rigid. Fusible fleece is often sold in precut squares or by the yard in widths of 45" (when sold by the meter, it comes in 90cm and 150cm widths).

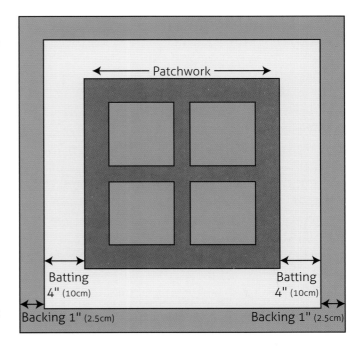

Batting. The batting you choose will often depend on what kind of loft—puffiness—and warmth you're looking for. Shown here (from left to right) are polyester, cotton, fusible fleece, and insulated batting.

Insulated batting: This batting is typically paired with projects intended for kitchen use, such as potholders and casserole covers. It reflects the temperature of the items placed inside it, keeping hot foods hot and cold foods cold. Like fusible fleece, this is also sold in precut packages or by the yard in widths of 45" (114cm).

Polyester: If you encounter a particularly puffy quilt, it probably contains polyester batting. This kind of batting tends to have a very high loft, which can make it difficult to quilt through, especially if the quilt is large. If using polyester batting, you might also encounter bearding, where the batting gathers and bunches inside the quilt, creating a tangled mess. This batting is not recommended for quilting unless you use the quilt tying method (page 67).

Batting can be purchased in pre-cut blanket-sized rolls or by the yard. Be sure to purchase batting that is roughly 8" (20.5cm) wider and longer than your patchwork so it will end up being 4" (10cm) larger on all sides. (The larger your quilt top, the more important it is to have at least 8 inches [10cm] of play, as the batting will shrink up during the quilting process.) If purchasing by the yard, check the width of the batting to be sure that it is wider than one edge of your quilt top by 8" (20.5cm). Then ask for a yardage length equivalent to the other edge of your quilt plus 8" (20.5cm).

Calculating batting. Ideally, you should purchase a batting section big enough to cover your quilt top plus 8" (20.5cm). Batting comes bagged precut in common blanket sizes, or you can pick out a bolt of batting that matches your quilt's width and order the appropriate length.

The color wheel. Using the color wheel as a quick guide can help you easily find beautiful matches to your favorite colors.

CHOOSING YOUR PALETTE:
Quilting Color Theory

Now that you've selected the type of fabric you'd like to use, next up is choosing the colors. You can purchase a fabric bundle or collection and let the designer do the coordinating for you, or you can learn a bit about color theory and select your own colors. Either way, these tips will make the decision as easy as possible.

COORDINATING PRECUT FABRICS

While fabrics for apparel and home décor are only sold off the bolt, quilting fabrics are used much like paints on a palette, so they're marketed and sold in lots of different ways. The fat quarters, fat eighths, precut squares, and precut strips described on page 17 can be found in bundles of coordinating colors, so all the matching is done for you, and they're an easy way to build up your fabric collection so it's beautiful, varied, and coordinated. Designer fabrics are often sold like this, allowing designers to show off an entire fabric collection.

Many quilt patterns will cater to these kinds of bundles, and this book is no different! Check the tip sections for each project to see how to use fabric bundles with the patterns.

SELECTING A COLOR SCHEME

If you'd rather choose your own color scheme than select fabric bundles that make the decision for you, there are some failsafe ways to get a fabulous-looking quilt without having to study the color wheel for ages.

Pick a star fabric: If you already have a fabric you're itching to quilt with, then you're in business! Simply use that star fabric and then choose complementary fabrics to match.

Monochromatic scheme: A really foolproof way to get a fresh and modern quilt is to go monochromatic. Choose one color that you adore and get fabrics in every shade of that color you can find. To add a fresh bit of contrast, bring in some white, gray, or black to go alongside your color as a clean background.

Complementary color scheme: If you want to take it one step further, a monochromatic color scheme with just a pop of complementary color (the color on the color wheel opposite the shade you've chosen) looks very sophisticated. Simply limit one block or section of your quilt to a complementary color and the purposeful contrast will look very artistic.

Analogous color scheme: Similar to the monochromatic color scheme, analogous colors are adjacent to each other on the color wheel. To keep it simple, limit yourself to just three or four colors and try not to vary the saturation (color intensity) too much.

GO YOUR OWN WAY

If you decide you want to try making your own color scheme, keep the following things in mind.

Create contrast: If you want to have colors in your quilt that pop, creating a focus color versus a background color, you need to choose your background fabrics accordingly.

Hues opposite one another on the color wheel contrast the most with each other. Warm colors (red, orange, and yellow) tend to stand out, while cool colors (blue, green, and purple) tend to recede.

Colors with high value (light colors) contrast with colors of low value (dark colors), making them both stand out more when used together than they otherwise would alone.

Saturated (intense) colors stand out more than their neutral (dull) counterparts. Gray and beige, and even white and black, serve as reliable neutral backgrounds.

Scale: Fabrics with large motifs (large-scale prints) are best used for large patchwork or, even better, for the back of your quilt. When cut up into small pieces, large-scale prints lose their context. Small-scale prints, however, are best used for small patchwork. When used in large areas, the details of small-scale prints get lost and they appear like solid fabrics.

Scrap quilt coordination: Even the most ragtag group of fabrics can seem to coordinate well if they're all bordered with the same matching fabric. Use this method to get rid of fabric scraps that don't seem to mesh!

Star fabric color scheme. After finding a fabric I absolutely loved and wanted to feature in my quilt—the raccoon print shown at center—I then developed a color scheme by finding fabrics that matched the accent colors within it.

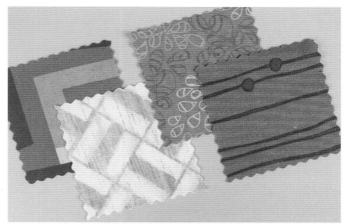

Monochromatic color scheme. Simply stick to shades of your favorite color and you've gone monochromatic!

Complementary color scheme. Add a pop of a complementary color to your monochromatic scheme and get an instant "dare to be different" artsy feel.

Analogous color scheme. Pick a range of a few colors that appear next to each other on the color wheel and you'll get a harmonious blended look.

Prepping Your Fabric

Now that you've purchased all of your wonderful fabrics, there are a few things you need to do to prepare them before you dive into your first project.

FABRIC ANATOMY

Selvedge: The outside machine-finished edge of manufactured fabric. It has a special weave and texture to it, making it different from the actual fabric yardage. It often has fabric information printed on it, such as the designer and color palette. Using the selvedges in your patchwork can lead to some complications, so it's best to trim them off.

Lengthwise grain: Also called the warp threads, this is the direction of the fabric that runs parallel to the selvedge edges. It carries the most strength and stability, as these threads don't stretch.

Crosswise grain: Also called the weft threads, this is the direction of the fabric that runs perpendicular to the selvedge edges, along the width of the fabric. These threads are slightly stretchy, but are still very stable.

Bias grain: This is the direction of the fabric that runs at an exact 45-degree diagonal between the lengthwise and crosswise grains (essentially from corner to corner of your fabric piece). Pieces cut on the bias will stretch significantly, making them useful for quilting only when curves are involved.

The most stable patchwork pieces will be cut on the straight grain, either the lengthwise or the crosswise one. Pieces cut at even a slight diagonal might stretch and cause you to end up with wonky patchwork.

GETTING READY

Pre-washing: If you've purchased fabric yardage, pre-washing is highly recommended. It pre-shrinks the fabric so it doesn't shrink more in your finished quilt; it removes the sizing (light starch) that can be found on retail fabrics; and it also washes out excess dyes that might leech onto other fabrics in your quilt or onto your clothes as you sew. I prefer to wash in warm water and dry with a cool setting. The one downside to pre-washing is that it will cause your fabric edges to fray, wasting a bit of your fabric. For this reason, you should not pre-wash precut fabric bundles, especially

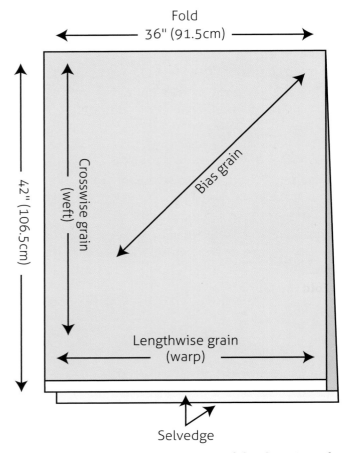

Fabric anatomy. Try to stay aware of the direction of the grain of your fabric while cutting. This will ensure that your patchwork pieces don't stretch out while you sew.

strips and small squares. Otherwise, you'll end up with a bundle of snarled threads in your washing machine and hardly any fabric at all!

Ironing: If your fabric has been pre-washed or simply has wrinkles from the store, you'll want to iron it so it's prepared for cutting. A spritz of water from a spray bottle will help steam out the wrinkles quickly.

Truing up: Before your fabric yardage can be cut into precise strips and squares, it will need to be trued. This is the process of making sure your fabric edges are exactly parallel and perpendicular to the selvedges. If you're just starting out, you might want to bone up on your fabric vocabulary and check out how to properly use a rotary cutter (page 24) before embarking on this process.

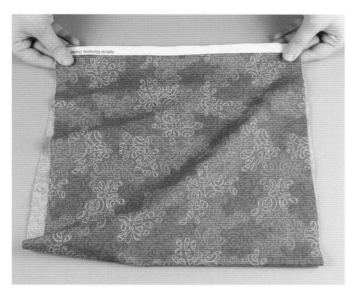

1. Fold the fabric. Fold your fabric in half lengthwise so the selvedge edges meet each other. You might notice that the fabric seems warped when you try to match the selvedges this way. This is very common.

2. Adjust the selvedges. Shift the upper selvedge edge to the right or left until the folded edge of the fabric is completely straight and smooth. You might notice that the cut edge of your fabric is now uneven— that's okay, it's what we're expecting. Turn the fabric so the uneven cut edge is on your dominant side. Now place your folded fabric yardage onto the cutting mat so the selvedge lines up exactly with one of the grid lines.

3. Place the ruler. Place your quilting ruler on top of the fabric. Position the long edge of the ruler perfectly perpendicular to the selvedge edge of your fabric; make sure the uneven cut edge of the fabric extends beyond the ruler on your dominant side. Use the guidelines on the cutting mat and ruler to make sure both your ruler and fabric are perfectly straight and aligned with one another.

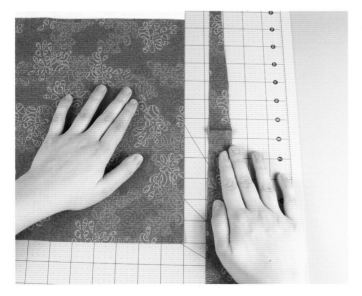

4. Cut off the edge. Cut off the uneven fabric edge by running your rotary blade along the ruler, moving away from your body (see Steps 3–5 of the rotary cutting sidebar). The cut edges of your fabric should now be perfectly perpendicular to the selvedge edges. You'll know you have it right when the cut edge of your folded fabric is perfectly straight and there is no kink at the fold. Once you've trued your fabric, any strips and squares cut from it will be exactly on grain.

ROTARY CUTTING

Making correct versus incorrect rotary cuts can mean the difference between perfectly straight, precise strips and squares and unfortunate finger cuts and nicked blades. Follow the steps below to use your rotary cutter in the safest and most effective way possible. Remember to use the safety latch and replace the blade as soon as it becomes dull.

● ●

1. **Position your fabric.** Fold your fabric in half lengthwise so the selvedge edges meet each other. Place the trued edge on your non-dominant side with the fold and selvedges parallel to one another. Strips are typically cut from the crosswise grain to be more manageable, although they can also be cut on the lengthwise grain for especially long pieces.

2. **Place the ruler.** Put your quilting ruler on top of the fabric. Align the horizontal measurement guides with the selvedge edge and folded edge of the fabric to achieve the measurement you need for your strip. You can typically cut through four layers of quilting cotton at a time.

3. **Position yourself.** Stand up, place your non-dominant hand on the ruler, and put steady pressure on it to hold it in place. Your fingers should be outstretched, but make sure none of them extend beyond the edge of the ruler.

4. **Cut the fabric.** Using your dominant hand, run the rotary cutter along the side of the ruler, moving it away from your body. Apply light pressure as you move the rotary cutter; the blade is much sharper than you think, and using too much pressure could actually cause you to slice off slivers of your plastic ruler.

5. **Remove the strip.** While still holding the ruler in place, set down the cutter and lightly tug on the fabric to see if it pulls away from the cut strip. If it's still attached, run the cutter over the fabric again using slightly more pressure. If your blade no longer cuts well, even when you're using the right pressure, you'll want to replace it.

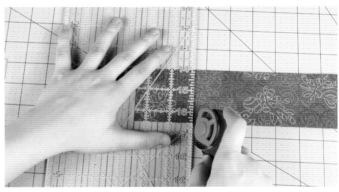

6. **Cut any squares.** To cut squares from the strip, turn it 90 degrees. Place your quilting ruler as before and trim off the rough edge of the strip. Then cut squares from the strip in the same way you cut strips from the main fabric.

QUILT ANATOMY: What Makes a Quilt?

In the bare-bones sense, a quilt is a type of blanket made by layering two pieces of fabric and sewing them together by stitching through both layers across the expanse of the fabric (called quilting). But the common quilts you see, and the ones that have been keeping us warm for generations, are those that comprise a sandwich of fabric, with two outer layers of woven fabric and a layer of batting in between. The quilt top is often made by piecing fabric scraps together. The quilting that joins the three layers is done for added strength and decoration.

A traditional quilt will have some common elements you can easily see from one example to the next, such as sashing, borders, and the like. You can decide to use these elements in your own quilts or go completely modern and throw the rules out the window. Feel free to combine elements to make the quilt of your dreams!

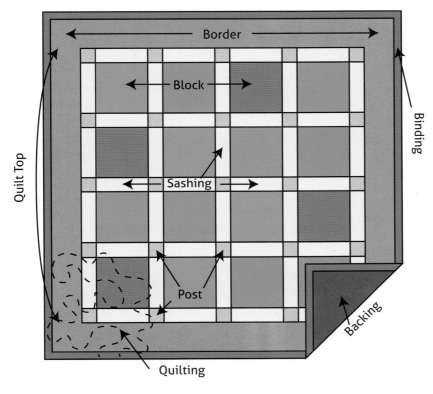

Quilt anatomy. These are the typical features you may see in a traditional quilt. Because we're going modern, feel free to use some of these, or none at all, to design your masterpiece!

Backing: The piece of cloth used for the back of a quilt.

Batting: The thin, fluffy material placed between the quilt top and the back to provide cushion and possibly warmth to the quilt.

Binding: The strip of fabric that binds the raw edges of the quilt top, batting, and backing.

Border: An outline sewn around the perimeter of a quilt to frame the blocks found inside.

Post: A contrasting block added at the intersection of sashing pieces.

Quilt block: A square of patchwork, often repeated in a grid-like design, that makes up the majority of a quilt composition.

Quilting: The stitching that anchors the three layers of the quilt and holds them together.

Quilt top: The side of the quilt that is meant to be prominently displayed. It may or may not be created from patchwork.

Sashing: A narrow strip added between quilt blocks to make the block stand out or as a way to provide the admirer with a visual resting place between blocks.

One-Block Techniques & Projects

It's time to build your quilting skills one technique at a time. Some techniques are a bit harder than others, but each one will build your skills and confidence until the quilting process no longer seems so daunting. Each technique is followed by an accompanying project to allow you to test your knowledge. Practice your piecing with a fresh and modern pillow cover (page 32), or learn about foolproof foundation piecing with a handy bedside organizer (page 38). Move on to other useful techniques like appliqué, quilt tying, machine quilting, and, finally, binding. Before you know it you'll be ready to tackle a full-size bed quilt! Let's get started with the first technique...

Following the Projects

The projects in this book are rated to reflect the complexity of the techniques used, as well as the overall time needed to create the projects. All of these pieces are completely approachable for beginners or confident beginners, but some are certainly easier than others. Here's how the rating works:

Perfect for those who are completely new to patchwork. It's good if you know just a bit about sewing, but it's not a requirement.

Ideal for those who have done a few sewing projects and understand some of the basic concepts of patchwork.

Good for sewers who feel pretty comfortable with simple patchwork and sewing and are ready to take things a bit further.

   In addition to the difficulty rating and techniques used, each project will indicate the materials and tools you'll need so you know what to shop for during your next trip to the quilt store. Then you'll be instructed about creating the patchwork from your fabric. The patchwork will be created using either pattern pieces and templates found in the book or squares and strips that you can easily cut without patterns. Once the patchwork is complete, you'll find instructions to guide you through the process of assembling the finished piece.
   You'll find loads of photographs and illustrations to help you with every step of the process, so you're guaranteed a gorgeous project every time!

TECHNIQUE:

Basic Piecing

The most fundamental technique in patchwork is piecing—the process of sewing small bits of fabric together to create larger fabric pieces by following a constant cycle of pinning, sewing, and pressing. The resulting pieces can be used in a quilt top, but they're also great for lots of other sewing projects. Patchwork can be done with loads of different shapes: squares, strips, triangles, semicircles, amoebas, you name it. But for beginners, straight seams, especially squares and rectangles, are the way to go. Don't think this will limit you—you'll be amazed by how many fantastic projects you can make using basic shapes! So grab your machine, a bit of fabric, and your thread, and get ready to start! In this section, we will explore:

- **Simple strip and square piecing:** Sewing together rectangular strips and squares.
- **Foundation piecing:** Using a paper foundation as a sewing guide for quick and easy piecing.
- **Fusible web and freezer paper appliqué:** Sewing one fabric shape on top of a background fabric as embellishment.

THE ¼" (6MM) SEAM

Why ¼" (6mm)? In patchwork, ¼" (6mm) seam allowances are standard when piecing fabric bits together. This was decided upon by quilters long ago because it lends just enough fabric to create a strong seam, but not so much that fabric is wasted. Almost every quilt pattern uses a scant ¼" (6mm) seam allowance when accuracy is a factor. It's possible to use a larger seam allowance by adjusting your pattern, as long as you keep it consistent while you sew. There are a number of reasons why you should be precise.

Accuracy for composition: In most quilts you see or make, every block is intended to be the same size and shape to obtain the desired look and composition. To achieve this, every fabric piece you cut must be precise, and every seam allowance you sew must be a scant ¼" (6mm). With precise cuts and accurate seam allowances, you'll create a quilt where every block is repeated perfectly.

Accuracy for fabric integrity: If your quilt blocks aren't accurate in size, you might end up with wobbly patchwork. As mentioned in the Fabric Anatomy section (page 22), fabric can sometimes stretch while you sew it, especially if your pieces aren't the proper size due to inaccurate cutting or seam allowances. Your finished quilt top won't lie perfectly flat; it will be wavy and bubbly, which is not a fun thing to tame.

All this scanty business: You may be wondering why the ¼" (6mm) seam is often called a "scant" ¼" (6mm) seam. This is because the turning of the fabric and the thickness of the thread use up just a hair's width of fabric. So if you sew a seam slightly smaller than ¼" (6mm) to account for this, your finished patchwork will end up perfect.

Sewing a scant ¼" (6mm) seam may sound daunting, but don't worry! There are loads of easy ways to get that exact scant ¼" (6mm) seam allowance without having to agonize over it.

- **Check your foot:** Your standard presser foot might already be a scant ¼" (6mm) from the needle to the edge. Simply tuck your ruler underneath your machine and measure out a scant ¼" (6mm) from the needle to see where it lands. If the presser foot is wider, try some of the other methods listed below.

- **Masking tape:** Tape a piece of low-adhesive tape (such as painter's tape or artist's tape) along the scant ¼" (6mm) mark.

- **Rubber band:** Wrap a wide rubber band around the free arm of your machine where the scant ¼" (6mm) mark lies.

- **Piecing foot:** If your machine didn't come with this foot, you could buy a compatible piecing foot, also called a ¼" foot. It comes with a ridge on the side that you can run the edge of your fabric against for the perfect seam allowance every time.

Testing your seam allowance: Once you have the tools in place to make a perfect seam allowance, it's time to test it out. To make sure your seam allowance is just right, measure the finished product and not the seam allowance itself. For instance, pin and sew together two 2½" (6.4cm) squares with the scant ¼" (6mm) seam. Press the newly sewn seam, and then press the squares open. Measure the two squares lengthwise down the center; you should get 4½" (11.6cm) total. If the measurement is longer, you'll want to adjust your seam allowance guide to create a slightly larger seam. If the measurement is shorter, adjust your guide to create a slightly smaller seam. Continue testing your seam allowance guide until you get it exactly right.

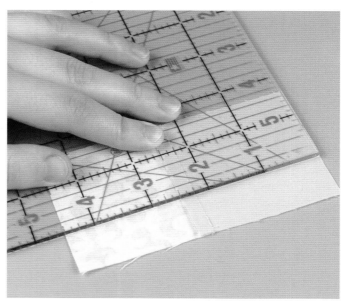

Measure your seam allowance. To be sure you have a correct seam allowance, measure the pieces after they've been sewn together and see if it all adds up right.

STITCH DYNAMICS

All you need to make fantastic patchwork projects is a simple straight stitch. This will be the workhorse of your piecing. Most machines will let you adjust the length of your straight stitch, usually by the millimeter, in a range of 0–4mm or 0–5mm. A length of 2–2.5mm is ideal for patchwork. Other machines measure in stitches per inch, which can range from incredibly tiny buttonhole stitches (90 stitches per inch) to long basting stitches (4 stitches per inch). A setting of 10–12 stitches per inch is a perfect middle range.

PRESSING SEAMS

After you finish sewing your first patchwork seam, you'll need to take it to your ironing station for the last leg of the pin, sew, and press cycle. Begin by pressing your finished seam right over the stitches with the fabric pieces still closed, with their right sides facing. This will set your seam, allowing the thread to sink into your fabric a little, and get rid of any puckers or warping you might have accidentally run in to. You can use a bit of steam if your iron has this option, but a quick spritz from a water bottle is a cleaner option, as the water doesn't have to travel through the iron's machinery.

The next step for pressing your seam is to open the fabric pieces you have stitched together and press the seam allowances either *open* or *to one side.* This step is hotly debated in the quilting community, as newer, modern quilters tend to press their seams open, and the traditionalists tend to press to one side. I personally prefer to press my seams open (particularly to reduce bulk), unless the patchwork behaves better with the seams pressed to one side. With certain techniques, like foundation piecing (page 36), you must press to one side because of the way the sewing is done. Try out some small projects, pressing the seams both ways, and see what you prefer. If you do decide to press your seams to one side, press them toward the darker fabric of the pieces you have sewn together; this will hide the seam.

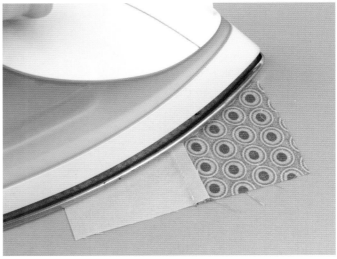

Seams pressed to the side. This is the more traditional method of quilting. Pressing to one side offers strength and "locked seams," but can create bulkiness.

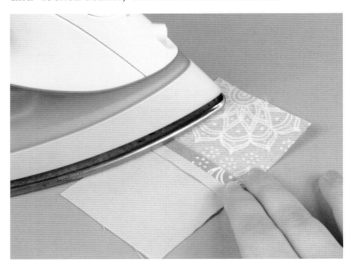

Seams pressed open. This method is often adopted by modern quilters. The seams aren't as strong, but they lie flatter and more predictably.

Pressing Pros and Cons

Pressing Open	Pros	Cons
	Patchwork lies flatter	More time consuming
	Less bulk	Not as strong
Pressing to One Side	**Pros**	**Cons**
	Easier to iron	Extra planning for "locked" seams
	Stronger seams	Extra bulkiness

LOCKING SEAMS

One of the benefits of pressing seams to one side, rather than open, is "locked seams." When you sew one row of squares with the seams allowances pressed to one side and another row with the seam allowances pressed to the other side, the joined rows have seams that butt together or "lock." To achieve this, you have to plan where to press your seam allowance so each row will lock effectively. Because it takes extra planning, you might see why improvisational modern quilters shy away from it.

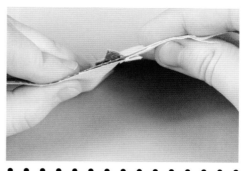

CHAIN PIECING

Perhaps the most useful trick that quilters may have in their arsenal is chain piecing. The process of pin, sew, press is very repetitive and time consuming, and one way to make it more efficient is doing all the sewing at once without all the thread clipping. Simply set up several pairs of pinned patchwork that are ready to be sewn and follow the process below.

1. Begin sewing your first pair of patchwork pieces together. Don't forget to remove the pins before they reach the presser foot!

2. When you reach the end of the first pair of pieces, leave them under your presser foot and get the next pair.

3. Tuck the new pair under the presser foot, leaving just a bit of space between the new pair and the old pair. Start sewing again, stitching the new pair together. Because you have not clipped the threads between them, the fabric pairs will be joined together in a short "chain." You may want to pull lightly on the first pair as you hold and stitch the second pair.

4. Continue in this manner until all the pairs are sewn together and joined in a chain.

5. When you've finished sewing, clip the threads between each pair to separate them from the chain.

Chain piecing. This simple trick consists of nothing more than tucking your next bit of sewing into your machine right after the previous one. The threads form a chain that can be clipped later.

Stylish Strips Pillow Cover

Try out your piecing skills with this simple pillow cover made from various fabric strips. The straightforward piecing method is a little improvisational and very simple to take on. Make one in your favorite colors for a fabulous pop of style on your bed or couch!

DIFFICULTY: ⬡

MAKES:
One pillow cover for a 16" (40.6cm) pillow form

TECHNIQUES:
Rotary cutting (page 24)

Piecing (page 28)

Double-fold hems

SUGGESTED FABRICS:
Quilting cotton, flannel, linen, poplin, voile, chambray, thin corduroy

TOOLS
Quilter's toolkit (see page 13)

Chopstick or similar turning tool

MATERIALS

FABRIC

Charcoal background fabric: ½ yd. (0.5m)

Green and blue focus fabrics: 1 fat quarter each

OTHER MATERIALS

Pillow form: 16" (40.6cm)

PRECUT PERFECT!

The focus fabrics can also be replaced by one roll of 2½" (6.4cm)-wide precut strips, such as jelly rolls. You'll need a roll of at least five strips, or get more to make a set of matching pillows!

CUTTING PLAN

Following the rotary cutting instructions on page 24, cut the following fabric strips along the width of the fabric yardage (or fat quarter). Then subcut the strips as directed below. Sort the pieces into the lettered units, labeling them with sticky notes if desired.

From the green fabric cut:

5 strips: 2½" x 18" (6.4 x 45.7cm) (A)

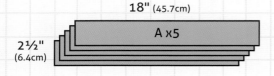

From the blue fabric cut:

5 strips: 2½" x 18" (6.4 x 45.7cm) (B)

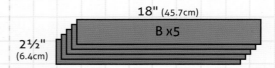

From the background fabric cut:

1 strip: 2½" (6.4cm) x width of fabric; subcut into:

- **5 random pieces:** ranging from 3"–7" (7.6–17.8cm) long (C)

- **4 strips:** 1½" (3.8cm) x width of fabric; then trim to 38" (96.5cm) long (D)

- **2 strips:** 1¾" (4.4cm) x width of fabric; then trim to 38" (96.5cm) long (E)

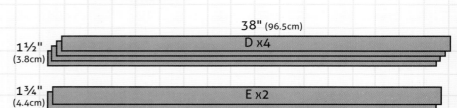

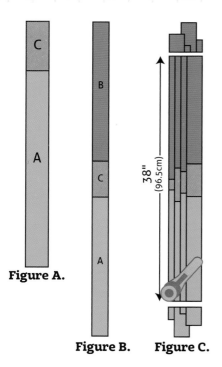

Figure A.

Figure B. **Figure C.**

PIECING

Use a scant ¼" (6mm) seam allowance for all seams. Press seam allowances open or to the side as desired; mine are pressed open.

1. Take a charcoal rectangle (C) and a green strip (A) and stitch them together along one short side (Figure A). Repeat this four times with the remaining C and A units so you have five pieced strips total.

2. Sew a blue strip (B) along the remaining short side of the charcoal rectangle (C) in one of the pieced strips from Step 1, creating one long strip (Figure B). Repeat with the remaining pieced strips from Step 1 for a total of five.

3. Stack the pieced A/C/B strips on top of each other. Place the center (C) sections generally together, sliding one or two strips out to the left or right for variation. Once the strips are staggered in this manner, trim all the strips in the stack to 38" (96.5cm) (Figure C).

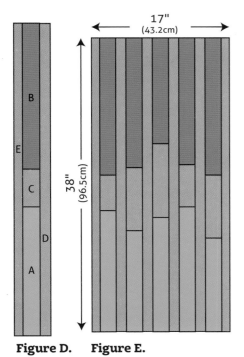

17"
(43.2cm)

38"
(96.5cm)

Figure D. **Figure E.**

4. Sew a charcoal strip (E) to the left long edge of a pieced A/C/B strip. Then sew a charcoal strip (D) to the right long edge of the pieced strip (Figure D).

5. Continue to build the quilt block working to the right. Add a pieced A/C/B strip, then a D strip. Repeat until the last pieced A/C/B strip has been sewn onto the right side of the block. Sew the last charcoal strip (E) to the right side of the last pieced A/C/B strip to complete the block (Figure E). The finished block should measure 17" wide x 38" tall (43.2 x 96.5cm).

QUILT IT!

Like the look of the block used for the Stylish Strips Pillow Cover project? Make it into a quilt by making multiple blocks and sewing them together. The math is all worked out for you in the chart on page 109. Use the chart to cut the pieces and assemble the blocks to form your quilt top. Then refer to the basic quilting guide on page 64 for the steps needed to finish.

ASSEMBLY

Follow the seam allowances as indicated in the instructions.

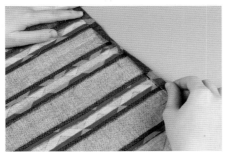

1 **Hem the top and bottom edges.** Fold one of the pillow cover's short edges over by ½" (1.5cm) onto the wrong side. Iron the fold in place. Repeat, folding the edge over by ½" (1.5cm) again and ironing the fold in place. Stitch along this fold to complete the double-fold hem. Repeat on the pillow cover's other short edge.

2 **Fold the cover.** Place the pillow cover right side up. Measure in 10" (25.5cm) from one of the short edges and fold the cover at that point so the right sides of the fabric are facing. Repeat with the other short edge, folding it over by 10" (25.5cm). The short edges should overlap in the middle. The folded cover should now be a square measuring 16" x 16" (40.5 x 40.5cm).

3 **Sew the sides.** Pin the open raw edges of the pillow cover together along each side. Using a ½" (1.5cm) seam allowance, sew along each raw edge with a straight stitch. Turn the cover right side out, poke the corners out, press the seams, and fill it with your softest pillow form.

TECHNIQUE:

Foundation Piecing

How would you feel if I told you there is a piecing technique so simple it feels like cheating? Using it, you'll be able to sew perfectly accurate seams without worrying about seam allowances, fabric grain, or measuring—and it's all done by sewing on paper! That's the beauty of foundation piecing, a technique more than 100 years old that uses a foundation (either scrap muslin or paper) as a sewing guide while you construct your quilt block. The foundation also acts as a stabilizer, making this technique perfect for off-grain fabric scraps and unconventional fabrics. We'll use paper; don't confuse this technique with English paper piecing or the foundation piecing done using muslin instead of paper.

A paper foundation pieced block starts with a pattern either traced or printed on a paper foundation—the block is typically constructed outward from a single (usually central) point. More and more fabric pieces are added by sewing along the pattern lines until the entire sheet of paper is covered. With foundation piecing, you can sew sharp angles and tiny shapes with complete ease!

THE PAPER

One disadvantage of foundation piecing is that it uses a lot of paper. There are many paper options to choose from, depending on your budget and preference. Thin papers tend to work better than thick papers, as the thin stuff is easier to rip away from the fabric once the block is finished.

Newspaper: The quilters of yesteryear used newspaper for their foundation piecing. With a good light box or window, you can trace your foundation pattern onto the paper and start sewing from there. Newspaper rips easily and sews well, but it cannot be run through your printer without risk of jamming and tearing.

Tracing paper: This is similar to newspaper in thickness, but is much easier to see through, making placing the fabric very easy during sewing. It does not work well with printers, though.

Printer paper: While not as easy to tear away as newspaper or tracing paper, printer paper is obviously easy to print on and cheap, if not free, because you can use the back of any scrap paper lying around the house: memos, letters, flyers, notices, or anything else you have on hand. For best results, use the thinnest paper you can find with as little ink on it as possible so it's easy to see through.

Foundation piecing paper: Quilt shops often sell a kind of paper specifically made for foundation piecing. It's much like tracing paper, but runs through your printer easily so making multiple copies is a cinch. The downside? You can't get it free the way you can scrap paper!

THE PATTERN

Finding a pattern: You can find foundation piecing patterns in books like this or online. Foundation piecing patterns show outlines of each segment with numbers that show the sewing order—just like a paint-by-number template.

Preparing your pattern: When you've found a pattern, you can trace it onto your chosen piecing paper using a light box or sunny window, or print it onto the paper using your home printer/copier. Digital patterns are easiest to work with because you can print them directly on your home printer—print as many copies as the project stipulates. Before you start sewing, trim your pattern generally around the cutting line, about ¼" (0.5cm) outside the line or so. If you're using opaque paper, consider tracing the pattern lines onto both sides.

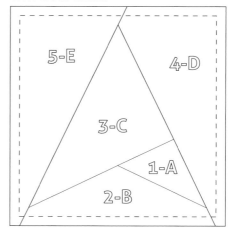

Foundation piecing pattern. A paper foundation pattern looks like this, with numbered segments to indicate the order in which you should add and sew your patchwork pieces.

THE PATCHWORK

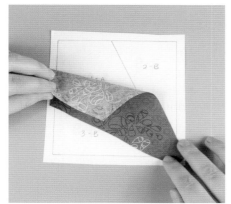

1 Cover the first section.
With the wrong side of the paper facing up, decide what fabric you want to sew on section 1. Cut a scrap of fabric at least ½" (1.5cm) larger than that section on all sides (bigger is better as a beginner). Pin it (or use basting glue) face up onto the paper pattern.

2 Layer the second fabric.
Look for where section 1 joins section 2; we're going to be sewing on that line. Cut a scrap of fabric for section 2 as you did for section 1. Pin it onto the fabric from section 1 (right sides together), lining up the raw edges so that they cover that sewing line.

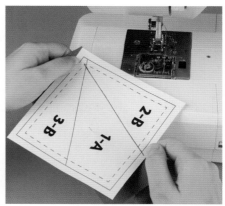

3 Sew along the guideline.
Turn the paper over, and sew along the printed guideline between sections 1 and 2 using a short stitch, about 1–1.5mm or 25–15 stitches per inch. This perforates the paper, making it easier to rip off later. Start about ¼" (0.5cm) before the sewing line and stop ¼" (0.5cm) after for insurance.

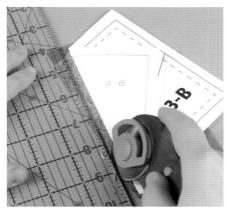

4 Trim the seam allowance.
Fold back the section 2 area along the stitching line and use your quilting ruler to trim the seam allowance down to ¼" (6mm).

5 Press the seam.
Open out the fabric pieces and press them as you usually would. If you look at your traced lines, you'll see that your second fabric now covers all of section 2.

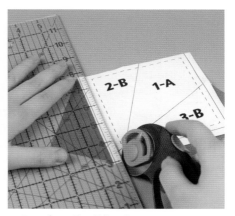

6 Trim the block.
Repeat Steps 2–5 for the remaining sections of the pattern. Finally, with the paper facing up, trim off the excess fabric along the cutting line. To finish, carefully rip the paper off the back of the block. Your quilt block is now complete!

Bedside Organizer

Try out foundation piecing while making this super simple bedside organizer. It includes a set of four pockets that can easily hold your nighttime reading material, glasses, tablet, or MP3 player. The added non-skid material will ensure it stays put between your mattress and box spring.

DIFFICULTY:

MAKES:
One 15" x 15" (38.1 x 38.1cm) organizer with four pockets

TECHNIQUES:
Rotary cutting (page 24)

Foundation piecing (page 36)

Applying interfacing

SUGGESTED FABRICS:
Quilting cotton, flannel, linen, poplin, voile, chambray, thin corduroy

TOOLS
Quilter's toolkit (see page 13)

Chopstick or similar turning tool

MATERIALS

FABRIC
3 different focus fabrics: at least 1 fat eighth each

Background fabric: ⅔ yd. (0.7m)

Lining fabric: ⅔ yd. (0.7m)

OTHER MATERIALS
Fusible fleece interfacing: ½ yd. (0.5m)

Non-skid material (such as rubber drawer liner): 14" x 12" (35.6 x 30.5cm)

Foundation piecing paper: enough for 9 patterns (9 printer sheets)

PRECUT PERFECT!

A 10" x 10" (25.5 x 25.5cm) charm pack can easily be used for the focus fabrics in this project. One 10" x 10" (25.5 x 25.5cm) square provides just enough fabric for the focus section of one block, so choose a pack of 9 to make the bedside organizer.

CUTTING PLAN

Gather the patchwork fabrics and, following the rotary cutting instructions on page 24, cut the following fabric strips along the width of the fabric yardage (or fat eighth). Then subcut the strips as directed below. Sort the pieces into the lettered units, labeling them with sticky notes if desired. Accuracy isn't crucial when cutting these rectangles, as they're just big enough to fit the foundation piecing sections. Then, cut the indicated pieces from the lining fabric and interfacing. Feel free to use a rotary cutter for speed and ease.

From the focus fabrics, cut:

1 strip from each color: 4" x 9" (10.2 x 22.9cm) (3 total); subcut into:

- **3 rectangles from each color:** 3" x 4" (7.6 x 10.2cm) (9 total) (A)

3 strips from each color: 5" x 9" (12.7 x 22.9cm) (9 total); trim each strip to 6" x 5" (15.2 x 12.7cm) (9 total) (C)

From the background fabric cut:

5 strips: 4" (10.2cm) x width of fabric; subcut into:

- **9 rectangles:** 6" x 4" (15.2 x 10.2cm) (B)

- **9 rectangles:** 7" x 4" (17.8 x 10.2cm) (D)

- **9 rectangles:** 8" x 4" (20.3 x 10.2cm) (E)

From the lining fabric cut:

2 rectangles: 16¼" x 6" (41.2 x 15.2cm) (Front pocket lining/back pocket base)

2 rectangles: 16¼" x 11" (41.2 x 27.9cm) (Back pocket lining/back base)

1 rectangle: 16¼" x 16 (41.2 x 40.6cm) (Back lining)

From the interfacing cut:

1 rectangle: 15¼" x 5" (38.7 x 12.7cm) (Front pocket interfacing)

1 rectangle: 15¼" x 10" (38.7 x 25.4cm) (Back pocket interfacing)

1 rectangle: 15¼" x 15" (38.7 x 38.1cm) (Back interfacing)

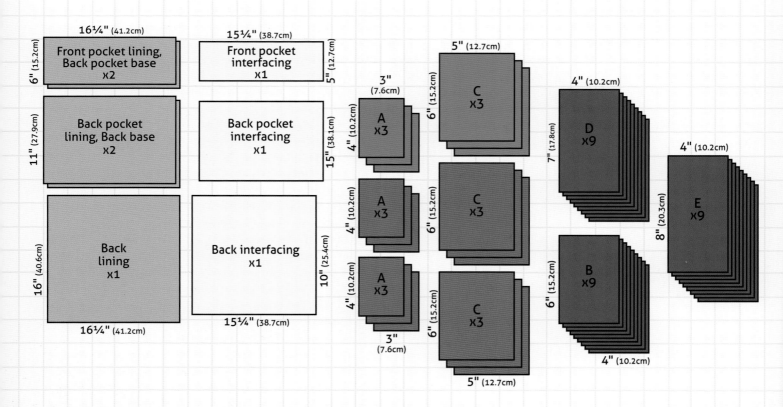

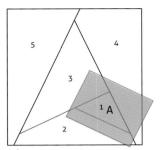

Figure A.

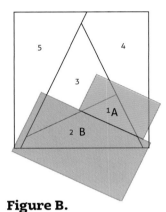

Figure B.

6"
(15.2cm)

E   D

C

A

B

5¾"
(14.6cm)

x9

Figure C.

x3

Figure D.

PIECING

Set aside the cut lining and interfacing pieces for now. Gather all the cut patchwork rectangles for piecing. Use a scant ¼" (6mm) seam allowance for all seams. Press seam allowances to the side following the foundation piecing method.

1. Following the guidelines for foundation piecing (page 36), pin a focus fabric rectangle (A) over Section 1 of the pattern found on page 124 (Figure A).

2. Add the smallest background rectangle (B) and stitch it to rectangle A for Section 2 (Figure B).

3. Add the larger (matching) focus fabric rectangle (C) and stitch it to rectangles A and B for Section 3.

4. Add the next largest background rectangle (D) and stitch it to rectangles A, B, and C for section 4.

5. Add the largest background rectangle (E) and stitch it to rectangles B, C, and D for section 5. Trim the block along the outer lines and rip off the paper as dictated in the Foundation Piecing section (see page 36). This completes one block.

6. Repeat Steps 1–5 eight times to create nine blocks total. The finished blocks should measure 5¾" x 6" (14.6 x 15.2cm) (Figure C).

7. Line up three of the blocks in a horizontal row in whatever configuration you like, matching up the 6" (15.2cm) long sides. Sew them together to create one row for the organizer (Figure D).

8. Repeat Step 7 with the remaining blocks to create two more horizontal rows.

ASSEMBLY

Use ½" (1.3cm) seam allowances for all seams unless otherwise indicated.

1 **Sew the organizer back and back pocket.** The organizer is made of three layers stacked on top of one another: the organizer back, the back pocket, and the front pocket. The front pocket is a single row of patchwork. For the back pocket, sew a row of patchwork to the top long edge of the back pocket base (shown). For the organizer back, sew a row of patchwork to the top long edge of the back base piece.

2 **Fuse the interfacing.** Center the front pocket interfacing piece over the wrong side of the front pocket. Note that the ½" (1.5cm) seam allowances extend beyond each edge of the interfacing. Fuse the interfacing in place with your iron. Repeat to fuse the back pocket interfacing to the back pocket piece (shown) and the back interfacing to organizer back piece.

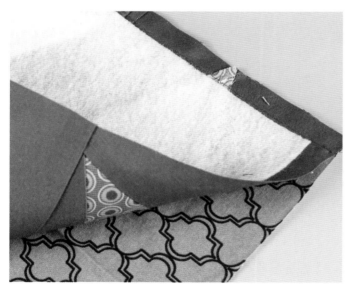

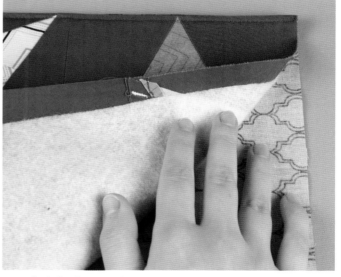

3 **Attach the lining.** Place the front pocket and front pocket lining pieces together with right sides facing. Stitch along the top edge to sew the pieces together. Repeat to attach the back pocket to the back pocket lining.

4 **Finish the pockets.** Press the seam between the front pocket and the front pocket lining. Then, fold the fabric along this seam so the front pocket and front pocket lining pieces are back to back with right sides facing out. Press this top folded edge and edge stitch along it for a crisp look. Repeat to finish the top edge of the back pocket.

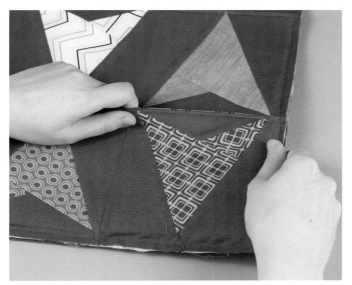

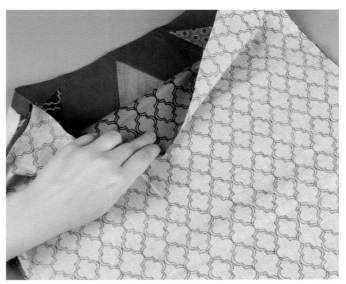

5 Baste the pockets. Place the organizer back face up on your work surface. Place the back pocket on top of it, face up, aligning the sides and bottom edges. Finally, place the front pocket on top of the back pocket, face up, aligning the sides and bottom edges. Baste the layers together along the sides and bottom.

6 Sew the back lining. Place the basted organizer and back lining piece together with right sides facing. Sew around the sides and bottom, leaving the top edge free for turning the organizer right side out. Clip the corners, turn the organizer right side out, and press it flat.

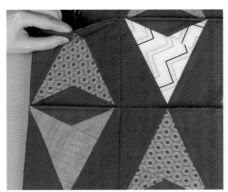

7 Sew the pocket separations. Because of the patchwork, your organizer will look like it has three rows and three columns. Sew a line along the right edge of the far left column on the front of the organizer to divide the pockets into two different sections.

8 Add the non-skid material. Fold over the fabric around the top open edge of the organizer by ½" (1.5cm) onto the wrong side and press the fold in place. Tuck one edge of the non-skid material about ½" (1.5cm) into the top opening. Edge stitch along the top edge of the organizer, sewing through all the layers to stitch the opening closed and attach the non-skid material.

QUILT IT!

If you liked the block from the Bedside Organizer project, you can also make it into a quilt! See the chart on page 111 for all the fabric quantities you need to make any size.

• • • • • • • • • • • • • •

Fusible Web Appliqué

Another quilting technique that will unlock loads more project possibilities for you is appliqué. It's the process of sewing one fabric shape on top of a background fabric as embellishment, and it's the perfect way to add curvy or detailed shapes that would otherwise be difficult to sew in patchwork.

The quilting world has dozens of ways to handle appliqué, but this book will cover two of the most flexible methods: fusible web and freezer paper (page 46). Fusible web appliqué is perfect for sewing especially tiny shapes that have sharp details.

SUPPLIES

For beautiful appliqué you only need a few supplies to get started. You shouldn't have any trouble finding these at your local fabric store or quilting shop.

Fabric: The same fabrics used for quilting can also be used for appliqué, though choosing a fabric that's as thin as, or slightly thinner than, your background fabric will make the job easier, as it will reduce bulk while you sew. Quilting cotton, flannel, thin corduroy, and batiste are all excellent choices. Felt is a great choice, too, and has the added benefit of not fraying along its raw edges. This is ideal for beginners because it requires little to no sewing.

Fusible web: Fusible web is a kind of paper-backed adhesive that, when adhered to your appliqué fabric, turns the fabric into an iron-on patch of sorts. Heavy-duty fusible web will hold your fabric in place indefinitely, with no sewing necessary. This works best for projects that won't get a lot of wear and tear. Light fusible web will hold your fabric in place temporarily so it doesn't shift or pucker while you sew it to your background fabric, making it ideal for quilts. You can find fusible web in precut sheets or by the yard.

PREPPING

Putting fusible web to use is pretty easy once you understand how it works. Gather up your appliqué pattern; even a hand-drawn doodle or outline will do. Note that this method will create a reverse image of your appliqué pattern, so be sure to flip images that are asymmetrical, text in particular.

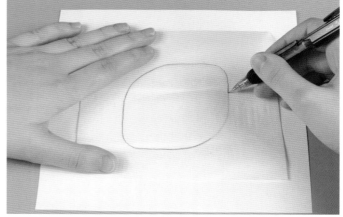

1 Trace the pattern. Your fusible web sheet will have a rough side (the adhesive side) and a smooth one (the paper side). Trace your appliqué pattern on the smooth paper side.

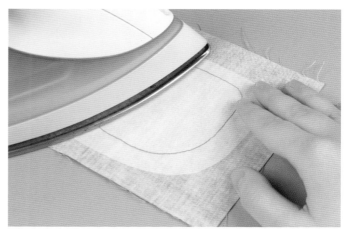

2 Iron the fusible web. Cut generally around the traced shape, then place the fusible web over your appliqué fabric with the adhesive side facing the wrong side of the fabric. Iron according to the package directions, usually by letting a medium-hot iron rest in place for a few seconds.

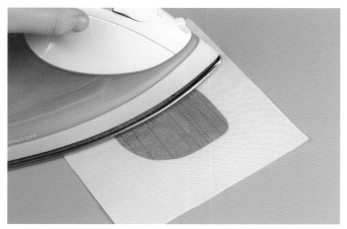

3 Iron the appliqué. Cut along the traced lines of your pattern. Peel off the paper, leaving the adhesive behind. Iron the embellishment with the adhesive facing the right side of your project fabric. If you've used heavy-duty fusible web, you can leave your project as is. If you've used lightweight fusible web, you'll need to sew the edge of the appliqué to reinforce it.

SEWING

Straight stitch: Using a regular presser foot, sew around the outline of your appliqué piece using a straight stitch about ⅟₁₆"–⅛" (2–3mm) away from the raw edge. This takes some careful coordination, so don't be afraid to stop and rotate your work when necessary. This method will leave your appliqué with exposed raw edges, so unless you want that look, use felt, which won't fray.

Zigzag stitch: You can also sew around your appliqué with a medium-width zigzag stitch that's 1–1.5mm long. This will encase the raw edges of your fabric in thread so it's less likely to fray over time. Align the zigzag so the outside edge of the stitch is just outside the appliqué edge—this should completely cover the raw edge. Be sure to stop and pivot at corners with the needle down, so the stitches look neater.

Straight stitch. A straight stitch around your appliqué piece is a simple and fast technique, but might leave some ragged edges on quilting cotton.

Zigzag stitch. A zigzag stitch takes a bit longer, but will cover the raw edges of your appliqué fabric, preventing any fraying.

TECHNIQUE:
Freezer Paper Appliqué

If fusible web appliqué wasn't quite up your alley, you'll be happy to know there's another form of appliqué that's also beginner friendly. Freezer paper appliqué not only avoids having to buy sheets and sheets of fusible web, it also looks much cleaner because all the raw edges are neatly tucked under the shape. Hand-turned appliqué is the hand-sewn version of this method, but the version I describe here is made fast and easy for machine sewers!

This type of appliqué works best for shapes without sharp curves or corners. Smooth, round curves are the ideal way to go. This method also lends itself well to large appliqué shapes, because it's reusable and more economical than fusible web.

SUPPLIES

Fabric: As with fusible web appliqué, a fabric that's as thin as or thinner than your background fabric is best. However, because the fabric edges will be turned under, try to steer clear of anything too thick that won't fold easily. Quilting cotton, chambray, voile, and poplin are ideal.

Freezer paper: Freezer paper is actually an amazing little product. It was originally used before plastic wrap and other food storage technology took off, but on fabric it does wonderful things. The waxy side of the paper, when ironed, temporarily adheres weakly to fabric. It's perfect for making templates or marking patterns, and then it can be easily peeled away; it's like a sticky note for fabric! Freezer paper can be found in dedicated quilt shops as well as in grocery stores.

PREPPING

There are many ways freezer paper can help you with your patchwork, but to get perfectly turned appliqué here's what you'll need to do:

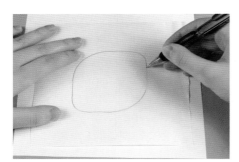

1 Trace the pattern. The sheet of freezer paper will have a waxy side (the shiny one) and a paper side (which is matte). Trace your appliqué pattern on the paper side.

2 Iron the freezer paper. Cut out the traced shape, then iron it with the waxy side facing down onto the wrong side of your appliqué fabric. Let the iron, set at medium to high heat, rest on top of the freezer paper for a few seconds without steam to adhere it in place. The paper shouldn't fall off when you finish.

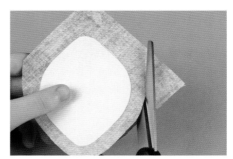

3 Cut the fabric shape. Cut around the appliqué pattern, giving yourself a ½" (1.5cm) seam allowance or so (you can cut smaller as you gain experience).

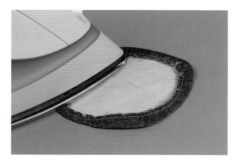

4 Gather the seam allowance. Run a basting stitch—either by hand or by machine—around the perimeter of the seam allowance you've given yourself. When you make it all the way around, tighten the thread so the fabric bunches up and around the paper pattern.

5 Press the gathers. The gathering will help create smooth curves around the rounded portions of your pattern; use the iron to press those in place until they're perfectly flat. When finished, remove the paper carefully without ruining the folds. You're now ready to sew!

SEWING

Once the turning is done, how you sew your appliqué is open to your imagination! You don't have to worry about frayed edges, so any stitch you like will work. Here are a few stitch suggestions. Be sure to pin or glue baste the appliqué in place where you need it so you know it's smoothly held in place.

Straight stitch: Using a regular presser foot, sew around the outline of your appliqué piece using a straight stitch about 1⁄16"–1⁄8" (2–3mm) away from the folded edge. This takes some careful coordination, so don't be afraid to stop and rotate your work when necessary.

Hem stitch: This stitch is usually used in sewing machines to perform a blind hem, but for appliqué, it's the one machine stitch that looks the least noticeable (especially if you use the right thread). The machine will stitch straight for a few stitches, and then go sideways to make one zigzag. Align the needle so it sews just outside the outer edge of the appliqué piece and takes the zigzag stitch onto the appliqué fabric.

Slip stitch: This hand-sewn method results in a nearly invisible seam. The stitch is done by taking a small 1⁄16"–1⁄8" (2–3mm) stitch into the fold of the appliqué fabric, then going across and taking another stitch from the background fabric. Repeat this process as you go around the appliqué shape, gently tugging the thread to tighten it. The threads should sink right into the fabric, nearly invisible!

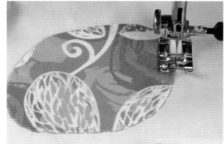

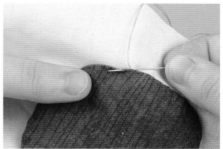

Straight stitch. Straight stitching around your appliqué offers a clean and simple look.

Hem stitch. A hem stitch is a slightly less visible machine stitch for your appliqué.

Slip stitch. A hand-sewn slip stitch is the ultimate way to make sure the stitching on your appliqué looks invisible.

Nesting Fabric Boxes

Any sewer will tell you how easy it is to build up a stash of quilting fabrics after only a few projects. If you make yourself some adorable storage boxes, you can use up some of that stash and organize the rest in a snap! The large cube fits perfectly on any shelf and has sturdy sides to hold loads of fabric. Meanwhile, the medium cube is perfect for your tools, and the small cube is a great fit for your thread. And when they're empty, they fit inside each other so they can be tucked away easily.

MATERIALS

FABRIC

Various focus fabrics totaling: ½ yd. (0.5m) (L), ⅓ yd. (0.4m) (M), and ¼ yd. (0.3m) (S)

Background fabric: ¾ yd. (0.7m) (L), ⅔ yd. (0.6m) (M), and ¼ yd. (0.3m) (S)

Lining fabric: 1¼ yd. (1.2m) (L), 1 yd. (1m) (M), and ½ yd. (0.5m) (S)

OTHER MATERIALS

45" (114.5cm)-wide thin cotton batting: 1½ yd. (1.4m) (L), 1 yd. (1m) (M), and ⅔ yd. (0.6m) (S)

Medium-weight interfacing: 6" x 2½" (15.2 x 6.4cm) (L), 6" x 2½" (15.2 x 6.4cm) (M), and 4 x 2½" (10.2 x 6.4cm) (S)

Mat board/cardboard: Five 11½" (29.2cm) squares (L), five 9" (22.9cm) squares (M), and five 6½" (16.5cm) squares (S)

20" [50.8cm]-wide fusible web: ½ yd. (0.5m) (L), ⅓ yd. (0.4m) (M), and ¼ yd. [0.3m] (S)

Clear vinyl: 5½" x 3½" (14 x 8.9cm) (L), 5½" x 3½" (14 x 8.9cm) (M), and 3½" x 3" (8.9 x 7.6cm) (S)

Squares of freezer paper: 7" x 7" (17.8 x 17.8cm)

Basting spray

DIFFICULTY:

MAKES:

Three fabric box cubes: large (12" [30.5cm]), medium (9½" [24.1cm]), small (7" [17.8cm])

TECHNIQUES:

Fusible web appliqué (page 44)

Freezer paper appliqué (page 46)

Rotary cutting (page 24)

Ladder stitch

SUGGESTED FABRICS:

Quilting cotton, flannel, linen, poplin, voile, chambray, thin corduroy

TOOLS

Quilter's toolkit (see page 13)

Chopstick or similar turning tool

PRECUT PERFECT!

A 10" (25.5cm) charm pack is perfect for the focus fabrics in this project. The charm squares are big enough to fit the large circles and will guarantee an assortment of small circles as well. For the large box you'll want at least eight charm squares, four for the medium box, and two for the small box.

CUTTING PLAN

Gather the patchwork fabrics and, following the rotary cutting instructions on page 24, cut the following fabric strips along the width of the fabric yardage. Then subcut the strips as directed below. After the patchwork pieces have been cut, cut the indicated pieces from the lining fabric, batting, interfacing, and vinyl. Feel free to use a rotary cutter for speed and ease. Keep the pieces for each box together.

Large box:

From the background fabric cut:
2 strips: 13" (33cm) x width of fabric; subcut into:
- **5 squares:** 13" x 13" (33 x 33cm) (A)

From the lining fabric cut:
5 squares: 13" x 13" (13 x 13cm) (Inner sides & bottom)
2 squares: 12½" x 12½" (31.8 x 31.8cm) (Bottom insert)
1 rectangle: 7½" x 3½" (19.1 x 8.9cm) (Handle)

From the batting cut:
10 squares: 12" x 12" (30.5 x 30.5cm) (Inner sides & bottom)
2 squares: 11½" x 11½" (29.2 x 29.2cm) (Bottom insert)

From the interfacing cut:
1 rectangle: 6½" x 2½" (16.5 x 6.4cm) (Handle)

From the vinyl cut:
1 rectangle: 5½" x 3½" (14 x 8.9cm) (Card slot)

Medium box:

From the background fabric cut:
2 strips: 10½" (26.7cm) x width of fabric; subcut into:
- **5 squares:** 10½" x 10½" (26.7 x 26.7cm) (A)

From the lining fabric cut:
5 squares: 10½" x 10½" (26.7 x 26.7cm) (Inner sides & bottom)
2 squares: 10" x 10" (25.4 x 25.4cm) (Bottom insert)
1 rectangle: 7½" x 3½" (19.1 x 8.9cm) (Handle)

From the batting cut:
10 squares: 9½" x 9½" (24.1 x 24.1cm) (Inner sides & bottom)
2 squares: 9" x 9" (22.9 x 22.9cm) (Bottom insert)

From the interfacing cut:
1 rectangle: 6½" x 2½" (16.5 x 6.4cm) (Handle)

From the vinyl cut:
1 rectangle: 5½" x 3½" (14 x 8.9cm) (Card slot)

Small box:

From the background fabric cut:
1 strip: 8" (20.3cm) x width of fabric; subcut into:
- **5 squares:** 8" x 8" (20.3 x 20.3cm) (A)

From the lining fabric cut:
5 squares: 8" x 8" (20.3 x 20.3cm) (Inner sides & bottom)
2 squares: 7½" x 7½" (19.1 x 19.1cm) (Bottom insert)
1 rectangle: 5½" x 3½" (14 x 8.9cm) (Handle)

From the batting cut:
10 squares: 7" x 7" (17.8 x 17.8cm) (Inner sides & bottom)
2 squares: 6½" x 6½" (16.5 x 16.5cm) (Bottom insert)

From the interfacing cut:
1 rectangle: 4½" x 2½" (11.4 x 6.4cm) (Handle)

From the vinyl cut:
1 rectangle: 3" x 3½" (7.6 x 8.9cm) (Card slot)

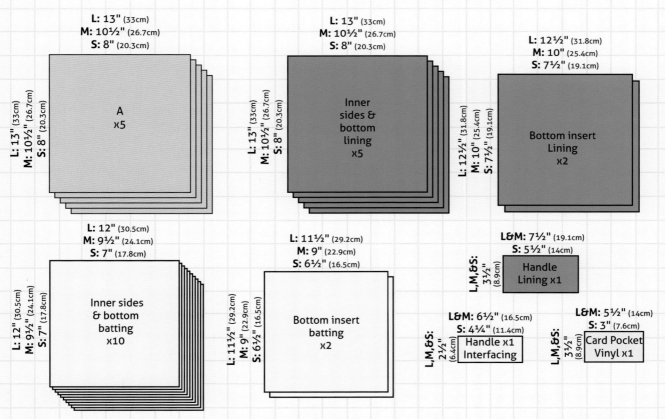

L: 13" (33cm)
M: 10½" (26.7cm)
S: 8" (20.3cm)

L: 13" (33cm)
M: 10½" (26.7cm)
S: 8" (20.3cm)

L: 12½" (31.8cm)
M: 10" (25.4cm)
S: 7½" (19.1cm)

L: 13" (33cm)
M: 10½" (26.7cm)
S: 8" (20.3cm)

A
x5

L: 13" (33cm)
M: 10½" (26.7cm)
S: 8" (20.3cm)

Inner
sides &
bottom
lining
x5

L: 12½" (31.8cm)
M: 10" (25.4cm)
S: 7½" (19.1cm)

Bottom insert
Lining
x2

L: 12" (30.5cm)
M: 9½" (24.1cm)
S: 7" (17.8cm)

L: 11½" (29.2cm)
M: 9" (22.9cm)
S: 6½" (16.5cm)

L&M: 7½" (19.1cm)
S: 5½" (14cm)

L: 12" (30.5cm)
M: 9½" (24.1cm)
S: 7" (17.8cm)

Inner sides
& bottom
batting
x10

L: 11½" (29.2cm)
M: 9" (22.9cm)
S: 6½" (16.5cm)

Bottom insert
batting
x2

L,M,&S: 3½" (8.9cm)

Handle
Lining x1

L&M: 6½" (16.5cm)
S: 4¼" (11.4cm)

L,M,&S: 2½" (6.4cm)

Handle x1
Interfacing

L&M: 5½" (14cm)
S: 3" (7.6cm)

L,M,&S: 3½" (8.9cm)

Card Pocket
Vinyl x1

L: 8 large circles
M: 4 large circles
S: 2 large circles

Figure A.

L: 32 small circles
M: 20 small circles
S: 8 small circles

Figure B.

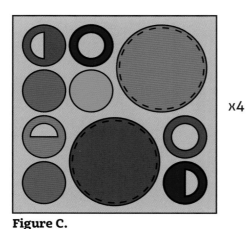

x4

Figure C.

THE APPLIQUÉ

Set aside the lining, batting, interfacing, and binding pieces for now. Gather all the patchwork pieces to complete the appliqué. The instructions provided are for the large box, with information about the medium and small boxes appearing in parentheses.

1. Following the guidelines for freezer paper appliqué (page 46), trace 8 (4, 2) large circles onto your freezer paper using the template on page 125. Cut out the circles and iron them onto your focus fabrics.

2. Trim about ½" (1.5cm) outside of each freezer paper circle to cut out 8 (4, 2) large fabric circles. Use the ½" (1.5cm) of fabric to hem the edges of each circle following the freezer paper appliqué technique on page 46 (Figure A).

3. Following the guidelines for fusible web appliqué (page 44), trace the following templates onto your fusible web: 8 (5, 2) small circles, 16 (10, 4) half circles, and 8 (5, 2) rings. Cut out the fusible web shapes and apply them to your various focus fabrics (Figure B).

4. Take 1 background square and arrange 2 (1, 1) of your large circles and 8 (5, 0) of your small circle pieces on top of it until you have a configuration you like.

5. Sew the appliqué circles in place on the background square following your chosen sewing method from the freezer paper and fusible web appliqué techniques (pages 46 and 44) (Figure C). For the large and medium boxes, repeat Steps 4–5 three more times with the remaining circles to create four sides for your box. For the small box, create a second side with 1 large circle, and then create two sides with 4 small circles each. The blank fifth side for all boxes will be the bottom.

ASSEMBLY

Use ½" (1.3cm) seam allowances for all seams unless otherwise indicated.

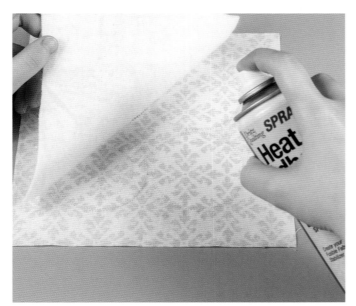

1 Spray baste the batting. Spray all the batting squares with a light coating of the spray basting adhesive. Apply a batting square to each of the five appliqué squares, five lining squares, and two bottom insert squares.

2 Add the card slot. Center the clear vinyl rectangle about 1½" (4cm) below the upper edge of one of the appliqué squares. Secure it in place with clear adhesive tape instead of pins to avoid leaving pin holes. Sew the vinyl in place by edge stitching along the sides and bottom.

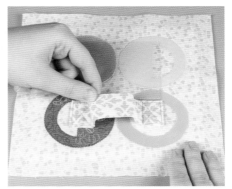

3 Begin the handle. Apply the handle interfacing to the wrong side of the handle piece. Fold the short edges over to the back of the handle by ½" (1.5cm) and iron the folds in place. Repeat with the long edges, folding them over by ½" (1.5cm) and ironing them in place.

4 Finish the handle. Fold the entire handle in half lengthwise with wrong sides facing. Edge stitch around the entire handle to finish it.

5 Attach the handle. Place the handle directly below the vinyl card slot, aligning the short edges of the handle with the bottom corners of the card slot. Sew the handle ends in place with a box stitch.

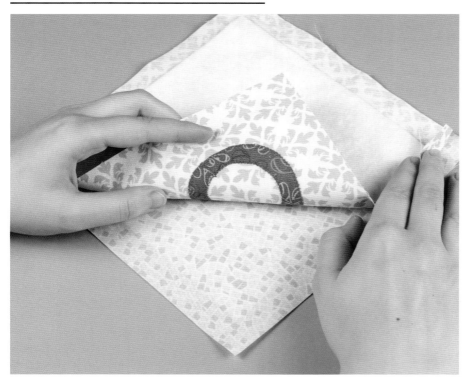

6 Attach the box sides. You will sew the appliqué squares to the bottom square to form the outer box. The trick to sewing a perfect box is to avoid stitching through the side seam allowances so there is fabric to sew the corners later. When attaching the squares, start sewing ½" (1.5cm) from the side of the squares and stop ½" (1.5cm) from the other side. To start, place an appliqué square and the blank background fabric square together with right sides facing. Stitch them together along the bottom edge, starting and stopping ½" (1.5cm) from each side. Repeat to attach the other three appliqué squares to the remaining edges of the bottom square.

7 Sew the lining sides. Repeat Step 6 with the five lining squares. When finished, the squares should form a plus sign.

8 Fold the top edges. Fold over the top edge of all four appliqué squares by ½" (1.5cm) onto the wrong side of the fabric. Repeat with the four lining side squares.

9 Sew the box perimeter. Place the outer box and lining together with right sides facing. Using a ¼" (6mm) seam allowance, sew along the inner corners of the plus sign shape, leaving the folded edges open. Clip the corners, turn the box right side out, and press it flat.

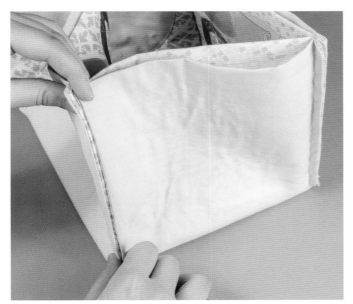

10 **Sew the corners.** Fold up two sides of the box so the lining is facing out. At the corner where the sides meet, align the sewn side edges and top edges Using a ¼" (6mm) seam allowance, sew the two sides together by edge stitching from the bottom to the top of the corner. Repeat to stitch the other three corners of the box. Turn the box right side out and poke out the corners.

11 **Create the insert.** Take the two bottom insert squares and fold over one edge of each square by ½" (1.5cm) to the wrong side. Place the two pieces together with right sides facing, aligning the folded edges. Sew around sides and bottom, leaving the top folded edge free for turning right side out. Clip the seam allowances and turn the insert right side out.

12 **Insert the cardboard.** Slip a cardboard square into the opening at the top of each box side and the bottom insert. Trim the cardboard if necessary to ensure a snug fit.

13 **Close up the openings.** Use a slip stitch to sew the top edges of the box sides and bottom insert closed. Tuck the bottom insert into the bottom of the box and you're finished!

QUILT IT!

If you liked the block used for the nesting boxes, try it out as a full quilt by repeating the block made for the large box. Use the chart on page 113 to cut the pieces and assemble the blocks to form your quilt top. Then refer to the basic quilting guide on page 64 for information on how to finish the whole quilt.

• • • • • • • • • • • • •

TECHNIQUE:

Piecing Triangles

Now that you've tackled a few projects with square and strip piecing, let's explore triangle piecing. This method specifically applies to right triangles. It's much the same as piecing squares because you're working with straight lines, but there are a few more factors to consider as you work along.

TYPES OF TRIANGLES

If you come across other quilt patterns that call for triangles, they might differentiate between half-square triangles (HSTs) and quarter-square triangles (QSTs). The difference has to do with fabric grain and bias based on the way the triangles are cut.

Half-square triangles: These are right triangles made by cutting a square in half diagonally from corner to corner. The legs of the triangle will be on the straight of grain while the diagonal of the triangle will be on the bias.

Quarter-square triangles: These are right triangles made by cutting a square into quarters diagonally from corner to corner. The legs of the triangle will be on the bias while the diagonal of the triangle will be on the straight of grain.

What does that mean for your quilt block? Ideally, your finished quilt block will have straight grain around all the edges for stability when you complete your quilt top. This is easy with square and strip pieces. With triangle pieces, it just means you have to consider the placement of your triangle's edges a little more carefully during piecing. The goal is to keep any bias fabric in small sections inside your block where it's manageable and doesn't affect your overall quilt.

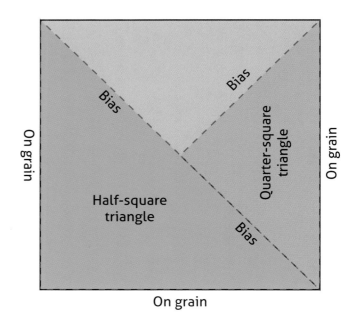

Triangles. Here's how you would cut half-square and quarter square triangles from a simple on-grain square of fabric.

MAKING TRIANGLE UNITS

Here are some super easy methods for creating half-square and quarter-square triangle units so you can easily make loads the next time a project asks for them. These are great for making chevron motifs, as you'll see in the accompanying project.

Half-square triangle unit. This method quickly makes two sets of half-square triangles. Start with two squares of fabric that are ⅞" (2.2cm) bigger than the finished triangles (without seam allowances) you need.

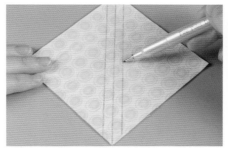

1 Draw the sewing lines. Place two squares together with right sides facing. Draw a diagonal line going from one corner of the square to the opposite corner. Draw a line ¼" (0.6cm) to each side of the center line as shown. These will be your stitching lines.

2 Create the triangles. Sew precisely along the stitching lines. When finished, cut along the center line to divide the units.

Quarter-square triangle unit. This method easily creates a quarter-square triangle unit that resembles an hourglass and is common in many quilt blocks. It starts with your finished half-square triangle units.

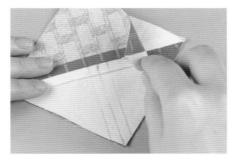

1 Layer the HST units. Place two half-square triangle units together with right sides facing. Position the units so the same fabrics are not facing each other. Then repeat Step 1 for creating a half-square triangle, drawing the center line and stitching lines.

2 Create the triangles. Repeat Step 2 of the half-square triangle technique as before, sewing along the stitching lines and cutting down the center line to separate the units.

Chevron Tablet Cover

Test your triangle piecing skills with this handy tablet cover. You'll find that combining right triangles can create some amazing designs, like this chevron. The tablet cover is the perfect combination of soft and sturdy, with batting nested inside and cardboard for stability. It even includes an inner pocket for charging cords or memory cards.

DIFFICULTY:

MAKES:
One 6" x 8½" (15.2 x 21.6cm) tablet cover suitable for 7" (18cm) tablets

TECHNIQUES:
Rotary cutting (page 24)

Triangle piecing (page 56)

Basic piecing (page 28)

SUGGESTED FABRICS:
Quilting cotton, flannel, linen, poplin, voile, chambray, thin corduroy

TOOLS
Quilter's toolkit (see page 13)

Chopstick or similar turning tool

MATERIALS

FABRIC

Green fabric: ⅛ yd. (0.2m)

Gray fabric: ¼ yd. (0.3m)

Yellow fabric: ⅛ yd. (0.2m)

Background fabric: ½ yd. (0.5m)

OTHER MATERIALS

45" (114.5cm)-wide thin cotton batting: ¼ yd. (0.3m)

Medium-weight interfacing: 5" x 3" (12.7 x 7.6cm) rectangle

Mat board or cardboard: two 8" x 5¼" (20.3 x 13.3cm) rectangles

¼" (6mm)-wide elastic: 12" (30.5cm)

Snap: ⅜" (10mm) metal sew-in

Basting spray

CUTTING PLAN

Gather the patchwork fabrics and, following the rotary cutting instructions on page 24, cut the following fabric strips along the width of the fabric yardage. Then subcut the strips as directed below. Sort the pieces into the lettered units, labeling them with sticky notes if desired. After the patchwork pieces have been cut, cut the indicated pieces from the remaining background fabric, batting, and interfacing. Feel free to use a rotary cutter for speed and ease.

From the green fabric cut:
1 strip: 2⅞" (7.3cm) x width of fabric; subcut into:
- **4 squares:** 2⅞" x 2⅞" (7.3 x 7.3cm) (A)

From the gray fabric cut:
1 strip: 2⅞" (7.3cm) x width of fabric; subcut into:
- **8 squares:** 2⅞" x 2⅞" (7.3 x 7.3cm) (B)

1 strip: 2½" (6.4cm) x width of fabric; subcut into:
- **8 squares:** 2½" x 2½" (6.4 x 6.4cm) (C)

From the yellow fabric cut:
1 strip: 2⅞" (7.3cm) x width of fabric; subcut into:
- **4 squares:** 2⅞" x 2⅞" (7.3 x 7.3cm) (D)

From the background fabric cut:
2 strips: 2⅞" (7.3cm) x width of fabric; subcut into:
- **16 squares:** 2⅞" x 2⅞" (7.3 x 7.3cm) (E)

From the remaining background fabric cut:
3 rectangles: 7" x 9½" (17.8 x 24.1cm) (Inner cover inner pocket)
2 squares: 4" x 4" (10.2 x 10.2cm) (Corner tabs)
2 snap tabs (see pattern on page 125)

From the batting cut:
1 rectangle: 12" x 8½" (30.5 x 21.6cm) (Outer cover)
2 rectangles: 6" x 8½" (15.2 x 21.6cm) (Inner cover)

From the interfacing cut:
1 snap tab (see pattern on page 125)

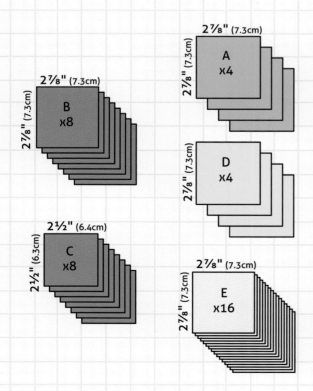

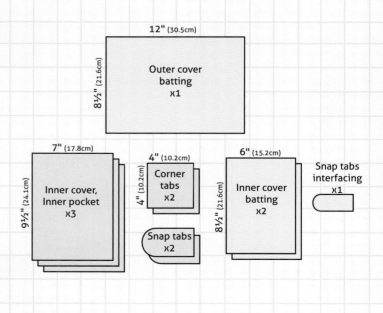

PIECING

Set aside the lining, batting, and interfacing pieces for now. Gather all the patchwork pieces for piecing. All seam allowances are a scant ¼" (6mm). Pressing seam allowances open is recommended here.

1. Following the triangle piecing technique (page 56), create:

- 8 half-square triangle units of green and background squares (A & E)

- 16 half-square triangle units of gray and background squares (B & E)

- 8 half-square triangle units of yellow and background squares (D & E) (Figure A).

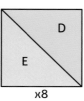

x8 x16 x8

Figure A.

2. Arrange the triangle units with the gray squares (C) as shown in Figure B to lay out the quilt block.

3. Sew the units together in rows, pressing the seams open or to alternating sides.

4. Sew the rows together to form the quilt block. If the seams were pressed to alternating sides, lock the seams together before sewing them (see page 31). If the seams were pressed open, match up the seams by pinning exactly through both seams before sewing them.

5. Trim the finished block to 13" x 9½" (33 x 24.1cm).

Figure B.

ASSEMBLY

Use ½" (1.3cm) seam allowances for all seams unless otherwise indicated.

1 Spray baste the batting. Spray all of the batting pieces with a light coating of basting spray. Apply the batting pieces to the wrong sides of their corresponding outer cover (patchwork) and inner cover pieces.

2 Create the snap tab. Apply the interfacing to the wrong side of one of the snap tab pieces, centering it. Sew the two snap tab pieces together with right sides facing, leaving the short straight edge free. Trim the seam allowances, turn the tab right side out, and press it flat.

3 **Attach the snap tab.** Finish the snap tab by edge stitching around the sides, leaving the raw end free. Then, baste the raw end of the snap tab to the left short edge of the outer cover, vertically centered, on the right side of the fabric.

4 **Baste the corner tabs.** Fold the corner tabs in half diagonally with wrong sides together to form two triangles. Align the raw edges of the triangles with the corners at one short end of one of the inner cover pieces with batting attached. Place the triangles on the right side of the fabric. Baste them in place by stitching along the raw edges.

5 **Baste the elastic strips.** Cut the elastic piece in half and place the halves on the short end of the inner cover piece, opposite the corner tabs, on the right side of the fabric. Arrange the elastic pieces going diagonally across the corners as shown. Baste the ends in place.

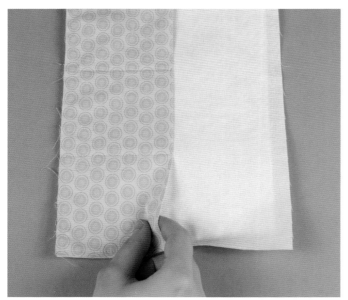

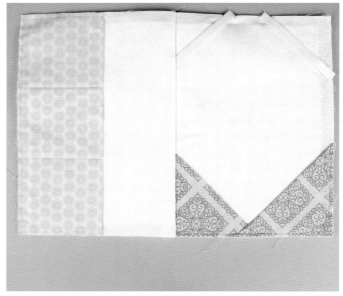

6 **Baste the inner pocket.** Fold the inner cover piece without batting (the inner pocket piece) in half lengthwise to create the pocket. Align the raw edge of the pocket with a long edge of the blank inner cover piece and baste the pocket in place. Sew two rows of stitches, each about 3¼" (8.5cm) from each short end of the pocket piece to create three sections for the pocket. Sew from the raw edge of the pocket to the folded edge.

7 **Join the inner cover pieces.** Place the inner cover pieces together with right sides facing. Stitch them together along the long edge without the pocket piece. Use a normal stitch for the first and last ½" (1.5cm) of the edge, but a long basting stitch in the middle. Press the finished seam toward the inner case piece with the pockets.

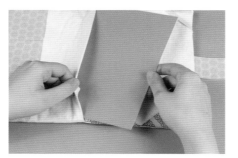

8 **Attach the outer cover.** Align and pin the inner and outer cover pieces together with right sides facing. Sew around the entire perimeter of the cover.

9 **Insert the cardboard.** Using a seam ripper, carefully rip out the basting stitches joining the inner cover pieces. Trim the seam allowances around the perimeter of the cover close to the stitching. Then turn the cover right side out. Press the seams, then slip a cardboard piece into each side of the cover.

10 **Close up the cover.** Pin the seam you opened between the inner cover pieces back up. Edge stitch over the fold to close the seam.

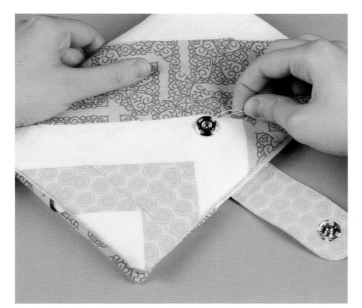

11 **Attach the snaps.** Sew the prong side of your snap to the end of your snap tab. Fold the tab over the cover and see where it comfortably rests on the front of the cover. Mark the location by pressing the snap into the fabric to leave a small indent. Use the mark to sew the socket side of your snap in place on the front of the cover.

QUILT IT!

If you liked working with triangles for this project, give it a go for a whole quilt! Simply repeat the block used to create the outside of the tablet case. Use the chart on page 115 to cut the pieces and assemble the blocks to form your quilt top. Then refer to the basic quilting guide on page 64 for information on how to finish the whole quilt.

• •

TECHNIQUE:
Quilting

After finishing your patchwork, the next major step in creating a quilt is called quilting. This is the process of layering your patchwork with some kind of backing material and typically a layer of batting in between, and then stitching through all those layers to hold them in place. This process not only holds all the layers of the quilt together, making it smoother, it also strengthens the quilt immensely, making it less likely to fray and fall apart over time. Once the layers are basted, they can then be quilted in lots of different ways.

Piecing the quilt back: If you can't find material large enough to fit your project as the backing, you'll need to piece your quilt back from cotton yardage. Get some tips below.

Quilt tying: Instead of stitching through the layers of your quilt, finish it more quickly using single knots tied through the layers.

Machine quilting: Stitching through the layers of your quilt with a sewing machine to create patterns of stitches over the entire piece.

Quilt-as- you-go: A non-traditional technique used to make quilting more manageable.

Planning Your Quilt Back

As you begin to consider making your first quilt, keep in mind that when the top is finished you'll need a quilt back as well. As stated in the Getting Started chapter, special extra-wide quilt backing material is available for large quilts. Quantities for extra-wide fabrics are given for the quilt projects in this book, but the limited colors offered might not work for what you had planned. If you want more options, you'll need to piece the quilt back from whatever fabric yardage you have.

PIECING

1. **Determine the quilt back size.** Measure your quilt top, then plan for a quilt back that's roughly 10" (25cm) larger both horizontally and vertically to account for any shifting that the quilt top might do as you sew (Figure A). (The larger your quilt top, the more important it is to have at least 10 inches [25cm] of play.) For this example, we will calculate for a 57" x 76" (145 x 193cm) quilt top; it requires a 67" x 86" (170 x 218cm) piece of fabric for the quilt back.

2. **Find your preferred quilt back material.** Decide what material you'd like to use for the quilt back. Quilting cotton is best here, as you'll want something sturdy. Measure the width of this fabric and subtract 2" (5cm) from this number to account for seam allowances. For quilting cotton that's 40" (101.5cm) wide (after trimming the selvedges and pre-shrinking), this becomes 38" (96.5cm).

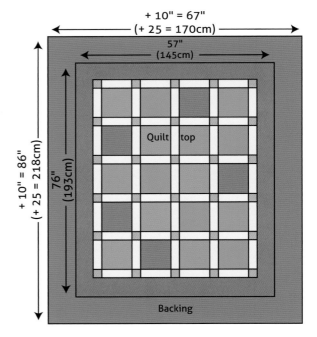

Figure A.

3. Divide your quilt width/length by this number.
Divide the width and length of your quilt back by the measurement derived in the previous step and determine which one has the smallest remainder. In our example, the calculations are as follows: 67 divided by 38 equals 1.76, and 86 divided by 38 equals 2.26. The side with the smallest remainder will be the direction where we spread the lengthwise grain of the backing fabric. Once calculated, round your answer down to the nearest whole number. For our example, to sew panels across the length of our sample quilt we would need 1.76 pieces, but across the width would require 2.26 pieces. We'll sew two panels across the width of the quilt and deal with the small gap in Step 5 (see Figure B). Your quilt back might not even have a gap—lucky! If that's the case, go ahead and skip to Step 6.

4. Determine the yardage. Multiply the measurement of the quilt going across the lengthwise grain by the rounded-down number calculated in Step 3. Divide this number by 36 for inches (100 for metric) to determine the amount you'll need for the majority of the quilt back. For our example, with two panels across the width of our sample quilt, you would calculate as follows for inches: 67" x 2 = 134"; 134" divided by 36 is about 3.75 or 3¾, so you will need 3¾ yd. For the metric system, 170cm x 2 = 340cm; 340cm divided by 100 equals 3.4, so you will need 3.4m.

5. Plan for the gaps. To fill in the leftover gap, this is where the magic of improvisational modern quilting comes in. Simply use scraps of fabric from the quilt top to make an interesting band of color for the back. Subtract the width of the main yardage from the quilt back requirement, add an extra 2" (5cm) or so for insurance, and plan to make a strip of patchwork by that width; perhaps try out some new quilt blocks or just go with simple strips (Figure C).

6. Assemble the back. Sew the large panels and contrast strip together with a ½" (1.3cm) seam allowance for added strength. Press the seams, and then use it for your quilt assembly.

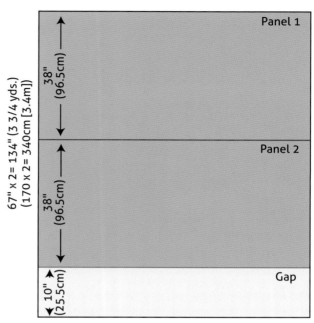

Figure B.

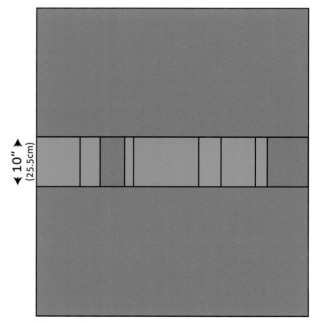

Figure C.

TECHNIQUE:

Making the Quilt Sandwich

The fundamental part of starting the quilting of your project, whether it ends up tied or machine quilted, is making the quilt sandwich. The tips here are ideal for handling especially large quilts so all the layers line up perfectly. Giving it your best effort during this step will ensure that the rest of your quilting goes smoothly.

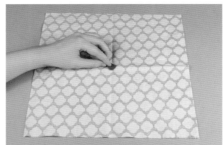

1 Fold the layers. Cut your backing fabric 10" (25cm) larger and your batting 8" (20.5cm) larger than your quilt top. Fold all sections into quarters to find the center lines. Note that the backing is folded with the right side facing out and the quilt top is folded with the wrong side facing out.

2 Lay out the backing fabric. Place your quilt backing fabric right side down on the biggest flat surface you have, such as a dining room table for smaller projects or a hardwood floor for bigger projects. Mark the center point with a pin or bit of masking tape.

3 Lay out the batting. Place the corner fold of your batting at the point you've marked in the middle of the backing. Using the center creases as guides, unfold the batting over the surface of the backing fabric. Remove the center marking from the backing and move it to the batting center.

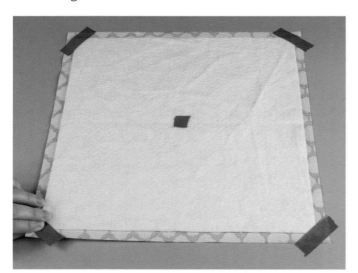

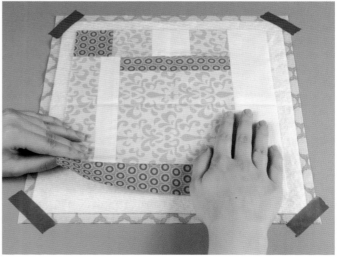

4 Tape the layers. Smooth out the batting and backing layers as much as possible; the edges don't have to align perfectly, but be sure to feel for any bumps or wrinkles. When finished, tape the edges of the batting and backing with painter's tape so the layers are taut.

5 Lay out the quilt top. Place the corner fold of your quilt top at the point you've marked in the middle of the batting. Using the center creases as guides, unfold the quilt top over the batting. When finished, smooth out the patchwork as best you can. There should be several inches of batting and backing extending beyond the patchwork.

TECHNIQUE:

Quilt Tying

Quilting your first project can be a little daunting, because you're basically layering three sheets together and trying to keep everything smooth while sewing them together all at the same time. Quilt tying takes away a bit of the stress by eliminating the need for quilting through rows of stitching—instead the stitches are replaced by single knots dotted throughout your quilt.

SUPPLIES

To sandwich your quilt for the first time, not only will you need your finished patchwork (the quilt top), but also the batting and backing fabric. Quilt tying is quite good at taming especially fluffy quilt batting, so feel free to break out this technique when you've got high-loft polyester.

Needle: In order to thread the string through your quilt, you'll need to find a long, strong needle with a big eye. Tapestry needles work fine, but in the quilting section of your store you'll find special needles designed specifically for hand-tying.

String: A quilt can successfully be tied with different kinds of strong material. Embroidery floss and pearl cotton (you may see it spelled perle, too) offer color selection, but aren't very colorfast. Thin yarns offer texture, but may not hold up well over time. Crochet cotton is considered the best choice. The fun part is looking through all the specialty yarns that can add a bit of pop to your project! No matter what you choose, make sure it will fit through the eye of your needle.

1 Mark the tie points.
Mark points on your quilt about 5" (12.5cm) apart in any configuration you like, such as a grid, a brick pattern, or centered in key points on your patchwork. (Instead of a ruler, you can also simply use your fist as a guide.) Either way, mark the points with large Xs using a fabric marker.

2 Thread the needle. Thread your needle with the string; leave one end long and fold the end at the needle's eye over about 3" (7.5cm). Working from the front of the quilt top, make a stitch at your first marked point, and leave a long thread tail. Continue jumping from X to X, making one stitch at a time until all the Xs are stitched.

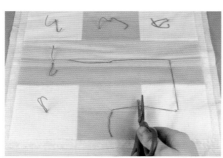

3 Cut the strands. Cut each length of string visible on top of the patchwork halfway along its length, making sure to leave the tails in place.

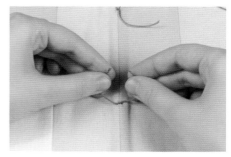

4 Make the knots. Tie each pair of tails into a sturdy square knot.

DIFFICULTY: ⬡⬡

MAKES:

One 6" x 26" (15.2 x 66cm) collar or
6" x 52" (132cm) scarf

TECHNIQUES:

Rotary cutting (page 24)

Foundation piecing (page 36)

Quilt tying (page 67)

Bagging out a quilt (page 73)

Filling stitches (page 73)

SUGGESTED FABRICS:

Quilting cotton, flannel, linen, poplin,
voile, chambray, corduroy, brocade,
velvet, fleece

TOOLS

Quilter's toolkit (see page 13)

Chopstick or similar turning tool

Clear tape

PRECUT PERFECT!

I found that a collection of fat eighths
works nicely for this project. Simply
cut 4" (10.2cm)-wide pieces off the
9" (23cm) side of a fat eighth for pieces
that are more than big enough to fit the
paper piecing pattern. The result will be
beautifully coordinated. You'll need at
least 6 fat eighths for a collar and 10 for
a scarf.

Braided Scarf

Have your first go at quilting by using the quilt
tying technique to make this snuggly scarf. The
foundation piecing pattern is specially designed
to be continuous, so you can repeat it and make
the scarf as long as you like! Repeat it three times
to make a cozy little collar or six times to make
a full luxurious scarf. This project is perfect for
using up irregular fabric scraps, or for trying out
some unconventional fabrics.

MATERIALS

FABRIC

5 (for collar) or 8 (for scarf) coordinating fabrics: ⅛ yd.
(0.2mm) each

Lining fabric: ¼ yd. (0.3m) (collar); ½ yd. (0.5m) of 60"
(152.5cm)-wide or ⅔ yd. (0.6m) of 45" (114.5cm)-wide
fabric (scarf)

OTHER MATERIALS

45" (114.5cm)-wide thin cotton batting: ¼ yd. (0.3m) (collar);
½ yd. (0.5m) (scarf)

String for quilt tying: 2½ yd. (2.3m) (collar); 4½ yd. (4.1m)
(scarf)

For collar: one 1" (25mm) button

For collar: 3" (7.5cm) of ⅜" (10mm)-wide ribbon

CUTTING PLAN

Gather the coordinating focus fabrics and, following the rotary cutting instructions on page 24, cut the following fabric strips along the width of the fabric yardage. Then subcut the strips as directed below. After the focus fabrics have been cut, cut the indicated pieces from the lining fabric and batting. Feel free to use a rotary cutter for speed and ease.

Collar:

From the focus fabrics cut:

5 strips: 4" (10.2cm) x width of fabric; subcut into:
• **21 rectangles:** 7" x 4" (17.8 x 10.2cm)

From the lining fabric cut:

1 rectangle: 7" x 27" (17.8 x 68.6cm) (Collar lining)

From the batting cut:

1 rectangle: 7" x 27" (17.8 x 68.6cm) (Collar batting)

Scarf:

From the focus fabrics cut:

8 strips: 4" (10.2cm) x width of fabric; subcut into:
• **39 rectangles:** 7" x 4" (17.8 x 10.2cm)

From the lining fabric cut:

1 rectangle: 7" x 53" (17.8 x 134.6cm) (Scarf lining)
2 rectangles: 7" x 14" (17.8 x 35.6cm) (Scarf pockets)

From the batting cut:

1 rectangle: 7 x 53" (17.8 x 134.6cm)

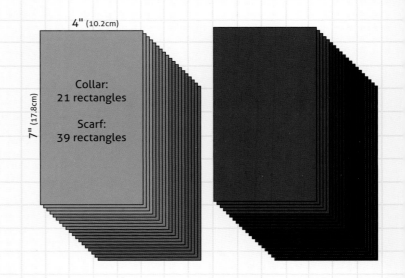

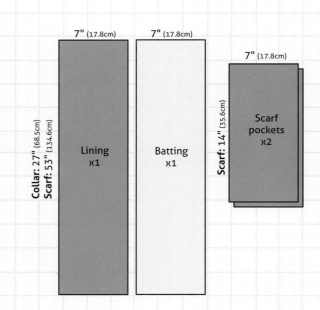

PIECING

Set aside the lining and batting pieces for now. Gather all the focus fabric pieces for piecing. All seam allowances are trimmed to ¼" (6mm). Seams are pressed to the side.

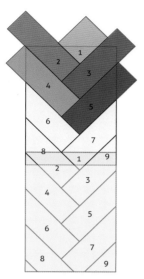

Figure A.

1. To make the collar, print/trace three sheets of the braid pattern on page 126; for the scarf, print/trace six sheets.

2. Take one pattern sheet and follow the foundation piecing technique (page 36) to begin sewing the focus fabric pieces together in the braid configuration. Stop after you add the piece to section 5.

3. Attach the next foundation piecing pattern sheet to the bottom of the current sheet, lining up the seam lines and pattern lines to continue the design. Starting with section 6 of the first sheet, continue sewing as before (Figure A). Repeat Steps 2 and 3 until you run out of sheets and have added all the necessary pieces.

4. Trim the pattern to the cutting line as described in the foundation piecing instructions (page 36) and tear away the paper pattern.

ASSEMBLY

Use ½" (1.3cm) seam allowances for all seams unless otherwise indicated.

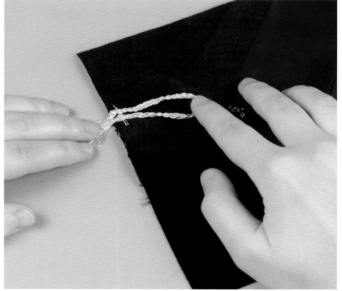

1 **For the scarf: Baste the pockets.** Fold the pocket pieces in half widthwise (bringing the short ends together) with wrong sides facing and iron them flat. Align the raw edge of each pocket with a short end of the scarf lining, placing the pockets on the right side of the fabric. Baste the pockets in place along the bottom and sides.

2 **For the collar: Baste the button loop.** Fold the ribbon in half to form a loop. Baste the raw edges to a short end of the collar, about 2" (5cm) in from the top long edge. Baste the ribbon on the right side of the fabric. Alternatively, I've made a braid of leftover tying string and used that in place of the ribbon.

3 Align the layers. Layer the scarf/collar pieces as follows: the batting, the lining (right side up), and lastly, the patchwork (right side down). Pin all the layers in place. Draw a 5" (12.5cm) line centered along one long edge of the scarf/collar. This will be the opening for turning later.

4 Sew the layers. Sew around the perimeter of the scarf/collar, skipping over the line you marked in the previous step. Trim the seam allowances at the corners, turn the scarf/collar right side out through the opening left for turning, and press the seams flat.

5 Stitch the opening closed. Using a ladder stitch, sew the opening in the side of the scarf/collar closed.

6 Quilt the layers. Following the quilt tying feature (page 67), stitch several knots throughout the scarf to anchor the three layers together.

7 For the collar: Add the button. Measure about 6" (15.5cm) from the short end of the collar without the ribbon. Then, measure in about 2½" (6.5cm) from the top long edge. Sew the button in place at this point.

MINI-LESSON: BAGGING OUT

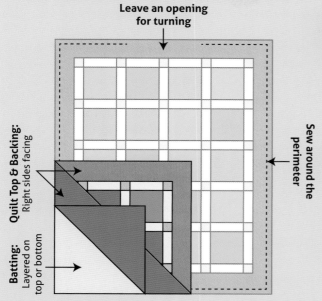

Leave an opening for turning

Quilt Top & Backing: Right sides facing

Batting: Layered on top or bottom

Sew around the perimeter

The technique shown in Steps 3–5 is called bagging out a quilt. It's a way of finishing the edges of the quilt without making a binding. This is the same method one would use to construct a pillow or a bag. It works wonderfully for very small quilts.

MINI-LESSON: FILLING STITCHES

In Step 6, you could also sew what are called filling stitches. These are small decorative hand stitches that take the place of quilting. Simply take a few stitches (instead of just one) in an X or perhaps a star shape. Then continue throughout the rest of the quilt.

QUILT IT!

If you enjoyed making the braided strip for the collar and scarf project, know that you can transform the design into a quilt just by repeating the braid strip over and over. Use the chart on page 117 to cut the pieces and assemble the blocks to form your quilt top. Then refer to the basic quilting guide on page 64 for information on how to finish the whole quilt.

TECHNIQUE:
Machine Quilting

Ratcheting up the complexity, machine quilting is a step up from quilt tying. While it takes a bit of practice to get used to working on a large canvas like a quilt, this technique has many possibilities.

PREPPING

See page 66 for info about making your quilt sandwich. After accomplishing that, instead of quilt tying, you'll baste the layers so the quilt can be taken to your sewing machine later.

When machine quilting, you need to have some way to temporarily hold the quilt layers together so everything stays flat and smooth when you take it to your machine. It's just like using pins with regular seams, but you need something a bit stronger and safer.

Safety pins: These are the go-to tool for most quilt basting. Regular safety pins will work just fine, but special curved safety pins for quilters are commonly seen in stores. They are available in a few sizes; select the one best suited to the thickness of your quilt. Simply pin through all the layers of your quilt about every 5"–7" (12.5–18cm) for even coverage.

Basting spray: Not all quilters like to use a basting spray, especially for bigger quilts, but for small quilts it makes the basting process quite easy. Mist the spray onto both sides of your quilt batting, then press it into your quilt top and backing as described in the quilt sandwiching steps on page 66.

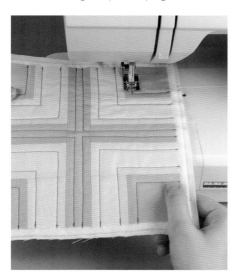

Outline quilting. This is done by quilting right alongside your seam lines using the presser foot as a guide. It's practically foolproof and looks fantastic.

STRAIGHT-LINE MACHINE QUILTING

The easiest way to break into machine quilting is to stick to straight lines. With some easy guides and a little bit of practice, you'll be working through your quilt in no time!

1. **Set up your guidelines.** Do yourself a favor and set up distinct guidelines beforehand so there's no question of where you need to sew when you start quilting. Ask yourself how much quilting you want and how many guidelines to use. Refer to your batting product information, which will usually give a maximum quilting distance before the batting runs the risk of bunching or bearding during washing. If you prefer puffier, comforter-like quilts, lean toward the high end of this maximum distance. Quilts with dense quilting (½" [1.5cm] apart or less) will last longer but will take much longer to finish. This will also shrink bed-sized quilts by a noticeable amount—around 1"–2" (2.5–5cm) depending on the density of the quilting. Here are two types of guidelines.

   - **Seam lines as guides.** Quilting right on the seams you've sewn for your quilt top is known as stitching in the ditch. While it's a common technique, bulky seams can work against you and often throw you off track. It's much better to try outline quilting, where you stitch just outside the seams (using the presser foot as a guide).

   - **Masking tape.** Straight lines that go across your quilt make a huge graphic impact that looks beautiful on modern-style quilts. Try using masking tape or painter's tape to run perfectly straight lines down your quilt.

2. **Install a walking foot.** As mentioned in the Getting Started section (page 10), a walking foot is a special presser foot that ensures an even feed of your quilting layers, preventing puckers and warping from the top layer down to the bottom. When doing straight line quilting, the consistency you get with this foot will really come in handy.

3. **Start sewing.** With your quilt all basted, marked, and ready to quilt, it's time to get it under your machine and get started. Use a slightly longer-than-average stitch (about 3mm or 9 stitches per inch) and a needle of a slightly larger size ($8_{0/12}$–$9_{0/14}$) to get through all those layers. You can use a strong neutral thread so the stitches blend into your quilt, or a contrasting thread if you want to show off your work. Now, here are some things to keep in mind.

Masking tape guides. For other straight lines, such as a diamond pattern, consider using masking tape to serve as guidelines that can be removed later.

- **Start from the middle.** While it's a little awkward, in order to prevent puckers and bunching it's better to start from the middle of the quilt and work your way out. In straight line quilting, you can start in the middle top of the quilt. If you encounter extra fabric while you sew, push it out to the edges of the quilt instead of letting it cause a pucker.

- **Let the puckers happen.** If you do encounter a pucker in your quilting and it can't be pushed to the side, instead of constantly pushing it downward and letting the problem snowball, it's best to just get it out of the way and sew over that little spot. It's better to have one little pucker and go on with smooth quilting than to have one large pucker and also warp your fabric.

- **Use previous quilt lines as guides.** Utilize every guideline you can while quilting, whether it be the side of your presser foot, the seam from your patchwork, or a previous quilting line. This will ensure that your lines look crisp and straight if you're going for a geometric look.

Quilting plan. When quilting, it's always best to start in the middle and work your way toward the outside to push out any extra fabric and prevent puckers. As the numbers here indicate, start in the center and work out to the right. Then return to the center and work out to the left.

FREE-MOTION MACHINE QUILTING

While usually considered a slightly more advanced form of quilting, free-motion quilting actually suits some beginners very well. Some people think it feels much more natural than other forms of quilting. It just depends on what kind of sewing personality you have—so give it a try if you feel adventurous. It might be the technique you were waiting for!

1. **Set up your machine.** Make sure everything is set up right on your sewing machine, and set it back when you're done.

   - **Install your darning foot.** This special kind of foot is meant for machine embroidery but also works for free-motion quilting. A little spring ensures it doesn't press on the fabric much at all, giving you exactly the right kind of pressure you need to free-motion quilt.

   - **Lower your feed dogs.** If your machine has this feature, you'll need it so it no longer moves the fabric for you, allowing you to take control. Most machines control the feed dogs through some kind of lever near the bobbin housing. You'll know you have it right when you see the feed dogs resting visibly lower than before.

2. **Find your comfort zone.** This is one of those techniques where you're just going to have to try it out first before you can hope to get the hang of it. Take a test quilt sandwich to the machine and try sewing on it, making little circles or meandering lines. The speed at which you move the quilt determines the stitch length, and the pressure you put on the foot pedal determines the speed of the needle. It's natural to want to go slower on the foot pedal when you're nervous, but you actually want to keep a rather consistent medium-high speed so your stitches aren't too long.

3. **Make a plan.** When you feel ready to start on your actual quilt, get an idea of how you want your quilting to look by researching some samples.

   - **Freehand quilting.** If you have a good rhythm, you can try just doodling stitches freehand. Stippling is the term used to describe meandering stitches that don't cross each other, and it's the easiest way for beginners to start. Then you can move on to other styles such as geometric stippling or fancier motifs.

   - **Quilting by pattern.** You'll see that free-motion quilting patterns run the gamut of simple straight lines to ornate filigree. These are definitely for when you feel more confident in your skills, but you can try designing your own quilting pattern by sketching on your quilt with a fabric pen or chalk, then stitching over the lines.

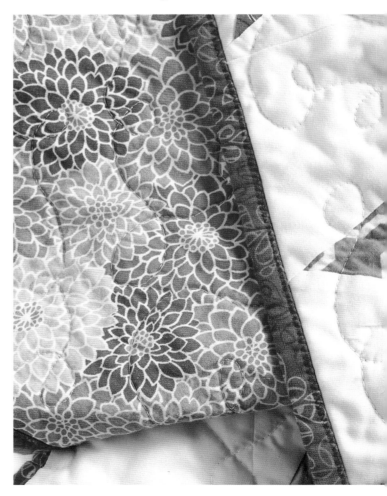

LONGARM QUILTING

You may have heard the term *longarm quilting*. A longarm machine is a very large sewing machine that works the opposite way a regular home sewing machine does: you move the sewing needle that's installed on a long arm across your stationary quilt rather than moving the quilt around underneath a stationary needle. Many say that this form of quilting feels more natural than working on a standard machine because it simulates drawing on paper. You can often rent out time to spend at a longarm machine at your local quilt shop, or they might have options for doing the quilting for you. They'll have certain specifications you'll need to follow, such as the size of your quilt batting and backing, so be sure to do a little research before you prepare those layers.

Stippling. The most basic form of freehand quilting, stippling is the process of quilting meandering lines that don't cross. As your skill progresses, consider tweaking this idea in different ways.

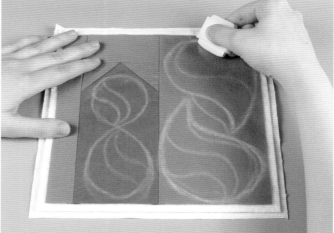

Quilting by pattern. Getting precise quilting stitches by following a pattern is a great goal to strive for as your skills progress. The projects in this book stick with the easier straight-line and freehand quilting, but you can try drawing outlines of your own designs to practice.

PROJECT:
Chain Block Purse

Try out your machine quilting skills on this basic tote bag that's been dressed up with purchased leather handles and a patchwork chain motif. The patchwork chain serves as an understated, classic accent for the bag, making it very fashionable. In addition, it's made extra sturdy through the use of fusible fleece interfacing, which you can quilt through to give your tote an extra design element.

DIFFICULTY:

MAKES:
One purse about 12" wide, 16" tall, and 2" deep (30.5 x 40.5 x 5cm)

TECHNIQUES:
Rotary cutting (page 24)
Piecing (page 28)
Machine quilting (page 74)
Strip sets

SUGGESTED FABRICS:
Quilting cotton, flannel, linen, poplin, voile, chambray, thin corduroy

TOOLS
Quilter's toolkit (see page 13)

MATERIALS

FABRIC

Cream background fabric: ½ yd. (0.5m)

Teal chain fabric: ¼ yd. (0.3m)

Seafoam link fabric: ⅛ yd. (0.2m)

Lining fabric: ½ yd. (0.5m)

OTHER MATERIALS

Fusible fleece interfacing: ½ yd. (0.5m)

2 leather handles: purchased

CUTTING PLAN

Gather the patchwork fabrics and, following the rotary cutting instructions on page 24, cut the following fabric strips along the width of the fabric yardage. Sort the pieces into the lettered units, labeling them with sticky notes if desired. After the patchwork pieces have been cut, cut the indicated pieces from the lining fabric and interfacing. Feel free to use a rotary cutter for speed and ease.

From the cream background fabric cut:
1 strip: 2½" (6.4cm) x width of fabric (A)
1 strip: 1½" (3.8cm) x width of fabric (B)
1 rectangle: 4½" x 36½" (11.4 x 92.7cm) (Left panel)
1 rectangle: 8½" x 36½" (21.6 x 92.7cm) (Right panel)

From the teal chain fabric cut:
4 strips: 1½" (3.8cm) x width of fabric (C)

From the seafoam link fabric cut:
1 strip: 1½" (3.8cm) x width of fabric (D)

From the lining fabric cut:
1 rectangle: 16½" x 36½" (41.9 x 92.7cm) (Purse lining)

From the interfacing cut:
1 rectangle: 15" x 35" (38.1 x 88.9cm) (Purse interfacing)

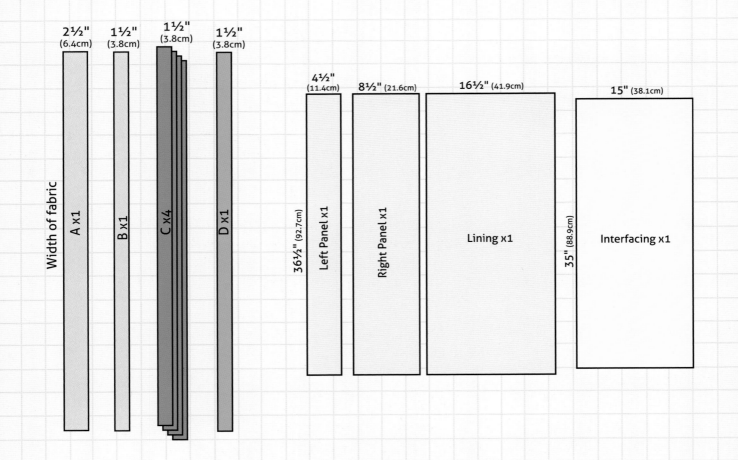

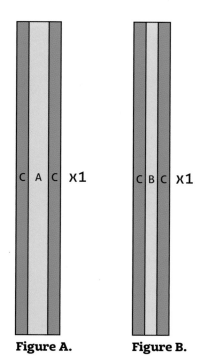

Figure A.   **Figure B.**

PIECING

Set aside the cut lining and interfacing pieces for now. Gather all the patchwork pieces for piecing. All seam allowances are a scant ¼" (6mm). Press the seam allowances open or to the side as you prefer; mine are pressed open.

Strip sets

Strip sets are an ingenious way to handle lots of small piecing without all the repetition. When a block contains a unit of pieces in a row that constantly repeat, you can often sew those pieces as a strip first, then subcut them into several rectangles, as we will do here.

1. Take the A strip and sew a C strip to each long edge, creating a long pieced strip (Figure A).

2. Take the B strip and sew a C strip to each side of it, creating another long pieced strip (Figure B).

3. Subcut the strips as instructed below. Sort the pieces into the lettered units, labeling them with sticky notes if desired (Figure C).

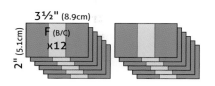

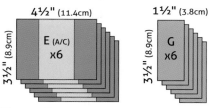

Figure C.

- **From the A/C strip set, cut 6 rectangles:**
  3½" x 4½" (8.9 x 11.4cm) (E)

- **From the B/C strip set, cut 12 rectangles:**
  2" x 3½" (5.1 x 8.9cm) (F)

- **From the D strip, cut 6 rectangles:**
  3½" x 1½" (8.9 x 3.8cm) (G)

4. To make the repeating chain motif, you need to construct two simple units, called Unit 1 and Unit 2. You already created the Unit 1 pieces in Step 3. They are the 3½" x 4½" (8.9 x 11.4cm) (E) rectangles you cut from the A/C strip set (Figure D).

5. To create Unit 2, sew an F rectangle to each long edge of a seafoam G rectangle. Repeat to create six of these units (Figure E).

6. Sew Units 1 and 2 together to create the chain block (Figure F). Repeat with the remaining units to create six blocks total.

7. Sew the six blocks together to create the accent stripe for the purse front and back.

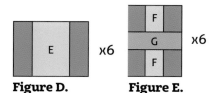

Figure D.   **Figure E.**

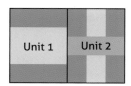

Figure F.

ASSEMBLY

Follow the seam allowances as indicated in the instructions.

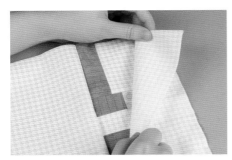

1 Create the outer purse. Sew the left panel to the long left edge of the patchwork strip using a ¼" (0.6cm) seam allowance. Repeat to sew the right panel to the right long edge of the patchwork strip.

2 Fuse the interfacing. Center the interfacing on the wrong side of the outer purse. There should be about a ¾" (2cm) margin on all sides for the seam allowance. Following the manufacturer's instructions, fuse the interfacing to the wrong side of the fabric.

3 Attach the lining. Place the lining and outer purse pieces together with right sides facing, matching up the short (16½" [42cm]) ends). Sew along both short ends using a ½" (1.5cm) seam allowance, leaving the long edges free. When finished, iron the seams and turn the purse right side out.

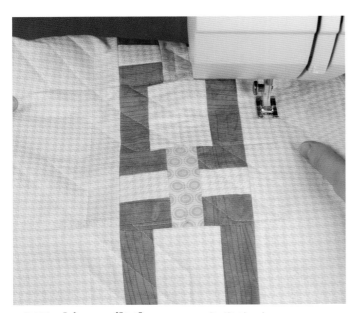

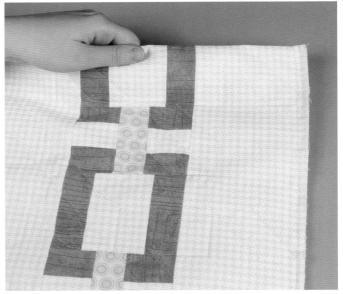

4 Machine quilt the purse. Quilt the layers together using a method of your choosing from the machine quilting feature on page 74.

5 Sew the purse sides. Fold the purse in half widthwise (bringing the short edges together) with wrong sides facing and sew along the raw side edges using a ¼" (0.6cm) seam allowance.

6 Finish the purse sides and bottom. Turn the purse wrong side out and press the side seams flat. Repeat sewing along the side edges, using a ½" (1.5cm) seam allowance this time. This should completely encase the raw edges of the previous side seams.

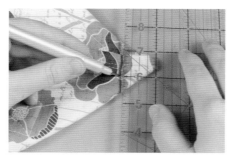

7 Sew the corners. At one of the bottom corners of the purse, fold the fabric at a 45° angle so that the side seam is aligned with the bottom seam and the corner creates a point. Measure in 1" (2.5cm) from the point and draw a line across the corner as shown. Sew along this line. Repeat with the remaining corner.

8 Define the sides. Turn the purse right side out. It should now have four distinct corners. Fold the purse so there is a distinct, straight crease going from the bottom right corner to the top right corner (parallel to the side seam). Edge stitch along this fold, about ⅛" (3mm) in. Repeat with the remaining corners, as well as the bottom edges. This will give the sides of your purse definition and structure.

9 Sew the handles. Place the ends of one handle on the top edge of your purse on the front side. Space the ends about 6" (15cm) apart and sew them in place. Repeat with the second handle on the back side.

QUILT IT!

If you like the look of the chain block used for the purse project, you can create a whole quilt by making rows of the chain block, separating them with sashing strips, and flipping every other row to achieve the brick tiling pattern. Use the chart on page 119 to cut the pieces and assemble the blocks to form your quilt top. Then refer to the basic quilting guide on page 64 for information on how to finish the whole quilt.

• • • • • • • • • • • • • •

TRADITIONAL TWIST

To give this project a more traditional look, try making one block that serves as an eye-catching focal point. The one shown here is a take on the traditional Weathervane block. Make yours in bold and fresh colors to give this traditional block a brand new twist!

• •

FABRIC

White focus fabric: ¼ yd. (0.3m)

Orange background fabric: ⅔ yd. (0.7m)

Lining fabric: ½ yd. (0.5m)

OTHER MATERIALS

Fusible fleece interfacing: ½ yd. (0.5m)

2 leather handles: purchased

TOOLS

Quilter's toolkit (see page 13)

CUTTING PLAN

From the white focus fabric cut:

1 strip: 2¼" (5.7cm) x width of fabric; subcut into:
• **8 squares:** 2¼" x 2¼" (5.7 x 5.7cm) (A)

1 strip: 2⅝" (6.7cm) x width of fabric; subcut into:
• **12 squares:** 2⅝" x 2⅝" (6.7 x 6.7cm) (B)

From the orange background fabric cut:

1 strip: 2¼" (5.7cm) x width of fabric; subcut into:
• **4 squares:** 2¼" x 2¼" (5.7 x 5.7cm) (C)

1 strip: 2⅝" (6.7cm) x width of fabric; subcut into:
• **12 squares:** 2⅝" x 2⅝" (6.7 x 6.7cm) (D)

2 rectangles: 3¼" x 11" (8.3 x 27.9cm) (Side panels)
1 rectangle: 16½" x 4½" (41.9 x 11.4cm) (Top panel)
1 rectangle: 16½" x 22" (41.9 x 57.2cm) (Bottom panel)

From the lining fabric cut:

1 rectangle: 16½" x 36½" (41.9 x 92.7cm) (Purse lining)

From the interfacing cut:

1 rectangle: 15" x 35" (38.1 x 88.9cm) (Purse interfacing)

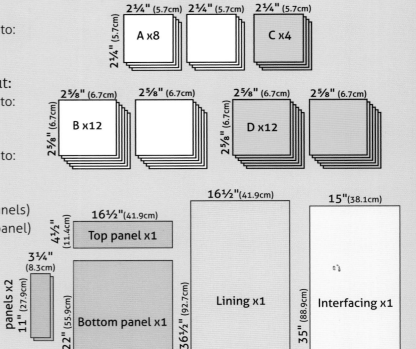

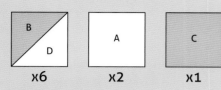

Figure A.

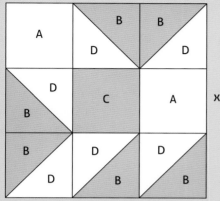

Figure B.

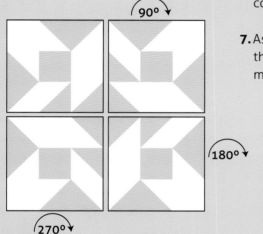

Figure C.

PIECING

1. Following the triangle piecing feature (page 56), create: 24 half-square triangle units of orange and white squares (B & D).

2. Gather six of the B/D triangle units, two of the white A squares, and one of the orange C squares (Figure A).

3. Arrange the squares in the configuration shown in Figure B.

4. Sew the squares together into rows, then join the rows to create the finished unit. Be sure to lock your seams (if each row's seam allowances were pressed to the side) or match up the seam lines (if the seam allowances were pressed open).

5. Repeat Steps 2–4 three more times to create three additional units.

6. Rotate each unit clockwise as shown in Figure C to create the four corners of the block.

7. As in Step 4, finish the block by sewing the top and bottom units of the block into rows, then joining the rows. The finished block should measure 11" x 11" (27.9 x 27.9cm).

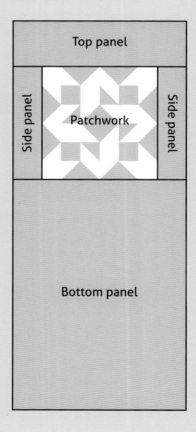

ASSEMBLY

Refer to the illustration at the right and Steps 2–9 from the assembly instructions on page 82 to complete the purse.

Sew the quilt block between the left and right panels using a ¼" (6mm) seam allowance. When finished, attach the top panel above it, and the lower panel beneath to create the configuration shown.

TECHNIQUE:

Quilt-As-You-Go Quilting

The quilt-as-you-go method is a nontraditional technique used to make quilting a whole patchwork project more manageable. There are a few ways to achieve it, but any approach that involves quilting sections of the quilt first and then adding more sections later can be considered a quilt-as-you-go method. This version is one I use the most myself to make creating extra-large quilts much easier.

PREPPING

Gather your choice of batting for the project you're working on. For this kind of quilting, thin batting is best, particularly cotton, or even just flannel yardage.

SEWING

Once you understand how this version of quilt-as-you-go is handled, you'll see it's quite a lot like paper foundation piecing because each part of the quilt works outward from the first piece, slowly getting bigger and bigger. For instance, in this example, imagine making a table runner from a row of quilt blocks using the quilt-as-you-go method.

When the strip is complete, you can simply trim away the excess batting and backing and bind it as you usually would, following the technique on page 95. You can also use this process on rows or columns of quilt blocks, working across or down a quilt to build it as you go.

1 Layer the first block. After you finish your quilt block (shown in purple), cut a piece of batting and backing fabric (shown in red) that's slightly larger. (You can use a second quilt block as the back instead.) Sandwich the batting with the quilt block and backing facing outward. Align all layers against the edge to the right. Quilt the three layers at this time.

2 Layer the second block. Working with a second set of pieces (consisting of another quilt block, batting square, and backing square), layer in this order: the new batting; the new backing, right side up (shown in blue); then the block quilted in the previous step, right side up (in purple/red); and finally the new quilt block, right side down (shown in green). Align all layers against the edge to the right.

UTILIZING QUILT-AS-YOU-GO

If you enjoyed doing the quilt-as-you-go method, you'll see how it makes creating extra-large quilts so much easier! The system I use for larger quilts when I don't have a lot of time or space goes like this; it's fast and also barely takes up any room under the machine's throat space.

1. Plan out your quilt in columns that are about 8"–20" (20–50cm) wide, whether that is by quilt block or a general section of your quilt. Cut your batting and backing accordingly.

2. Layer the first column of the quilt as you would for a whole quilt and quilt it with simple vertical machine quilting, such as straight lines or waves.

3. Using the quilt-as-you-go method, layer and quilt the next column of the quilt, then press the finished section. Run quilting stitches through the next section as you did for the first one.

4. Repeat Step 3 until all the columns of the quilt are complete, and then bind (see page 95) to finish.

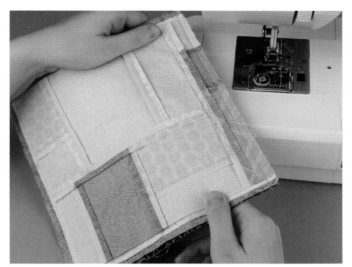

3 Sew the blocks. Sew along the aligned side of the quilt block through all the layers. Trim away the excess batting if possible to reduce bulk. The seams will still be a little bulky, but on the bright side, the previous block is already quilted and you can simply focus on the block at hand.

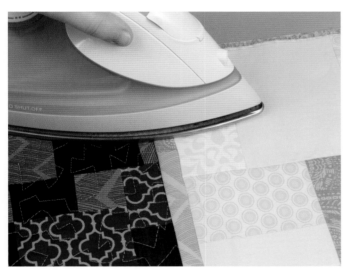

4 Press the layers. Press the second quilt block fabric away from the first, pressing the seam so everything is nice and flat. Quilt this new block, then repeat Steps 2–4 as many times as you like to get a continuous strip.

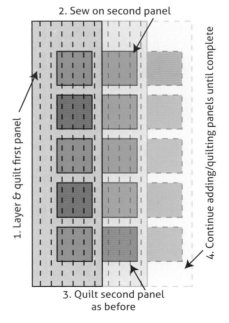

2. Sew on second panel

1. Layer & quilt first panel

4. Continue adding/quilting panels until complete

3. Quilt second panel as before

Large quilt-as-you-go-projects. By quilting only the right-most panel, one at a time, you'll never end up with more quilt under your machine than you can handle.

PROJECT:

Offset Squares Panel Curtain

This charming café curtain would make a perfect accent for any short window or the top of a doorway. The simple and sleek quilt block will perfectly blend in with your décor—a cheerful place for your eyes to rest without being overwhelming. Using the quilt-as-you-go technique, both sides of the curtain look finished and professional without a lot of extra effort. Make this in a light, breezy fabric and allow the light to shine through it for a beautiful opaque effect.

MATERIALS

FABRIC

Green focus fabrics: ¼ yd. (0.3m) total

Blue focus fabrics: ⅓ yd. (0.4m) total

Background fabric: 1 yd. (1m)

Backing fabric: 1 yd. (1m)

DIFFICULTY: ⬡ ⬡

MAKES:
One 36" x 22" (91.4 x 55.8cm) café curtain

TECHNIQUES:
Rotary cutting (page 24)

Piecing (page 28)

Quilt-as-you-go quilting (page 86)

Self-binding (page 94)

SUGGESTED FABRICS:
Quilting cotton, gauze, organdy, voile

TOOLS
Quilter's toolkit (see page 13)

PRECUT PERFECT!

A 5" (12.7cm) charm pack would work perfectly to replace the focus fabrics in this project, ensuring each square is nice and random! Each charm square easily replaces the 4½" (11.5cm) focus square you need, so get a pack with at least 18 squares for the curtain.

CUTTING PLAN

Gather the patchwork fabrics and, following the rotary cutting instructions on page 24, cut the following fabric strips along the width of the fabric yardage. Then subcut the strips as directed below. Sort the pieces into the lettered units, labeling them with sticky notes if desired. After the patchwork pieces have been cut, cut the indicated pieces from the backing fabric. Feel free to use a rotary cutter for speed and ease.

From the green focus fabrics cut:
1 strip: 4½" (11.4cm) x width of fabric; subcut into:
- **9 squares:** 4½" x 4½" (11.4 x 11.4cm) (A)

3 rectangles: 18" x 1½" (45.7 x 3.8cm) (Curtain ties)

From the blue focus fabrics cut:
1 strip: 4½" (11.4cm) x width of fabric; subcut into:
- **9 squares:** 4½" x 4½" (11.4 x 11.4cm) (B)

4 rectangles: 18" x 1½" (45.7 x 3.8cm) (Curtain ties)

TIP

For this project, you might have several fabrics for each focus fabric color. If this is the case, cut your 4½" x 4½" (11.4 x 11.4cm) squares randomly from each fabric. As long as you end up with nine squares total, it doesn't matter which fabrics you cut from.

• •

From the background fabric cut:
5 strips: 2½" (6.4cm) x width of fabric; subcut into:
- **18 rectangles:** 2½" x 4½" (6.4 x 11.4cm) (C)

- **12 rectangles:** 2½" x 8½" (6.4 x 21.6cm) (D)

3 strips: 4½" (11.4cm) x width of fabric; subcut into:
- **8 rectangles:** 4½" x 8½" (11.4 x 21.6cm) (E)

- **4 rectangles:** 4½" x 10½" (11.4 x 26.7cm) (F)

From the backing fabric cut:
1 rectangle: 40½" x 10½" (102.8 x 26.7cm) (Upper panel)
2 rectangles: 40½" x 8½" (102.8 x 21.6cm) (Lower panels)

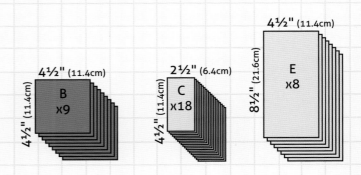

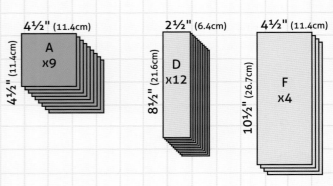

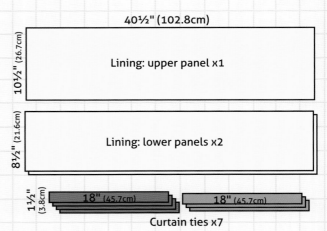

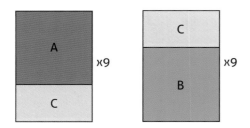

Figure A.

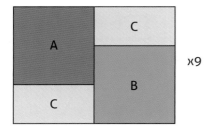

Figure B.

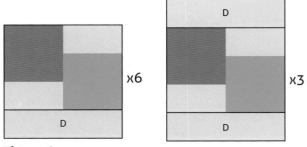

Figure C.

PIECING

Set aside the cut backing pieces for now. Gather all the patchwork pieces for piecing. All seam allowances are a scant ¼" (6mm). Press the seams allowances open or to the side as you prefer; mine are pressed open.

1. Sew an A square to one long edge of a C rectangle, creating a Unit 1 piece. Repeat to create nine Unit 1 pieces total. Sew a B square to one long edge of a C rectangle, creating a Unit 2 piece. Repeat to create nine Unit 2 pieces (Figure A).

2. Sew together a Unit 1 piece and a Unit 2 piece as shown in Figure B to create an offset square block. Repeat this eight more times to create nine blocks total (Figure B).

3. For three of the blocks, sew a D horizontal sashing rectangle to the top and bottom. For the remaining six blocks, sew a D horizontal sashing rectangle to the bottom only (Figure C).

4. Sew the three tall 10½" (26.7cm) blocks together in a row with F sashing rectangles between each one and on the ends of the row. Sew three short 8½" (21.6cm) blocks together in a row with E sashing rectangles between each one and on the ends of the row. Repeat to create a second short row (Figure D).

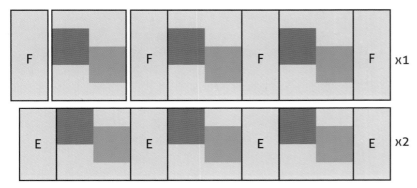

Figure D.

ASSEMBLY

Seam allowances are ¼" (6mm) unless otherwise indicated in the instructions.

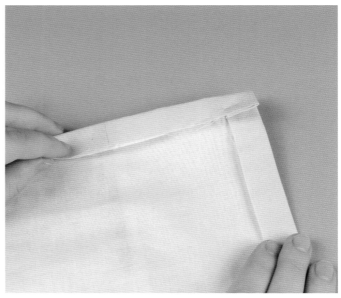

1 **Join the curtain rows.** Use the quilt-as-you-go technique from the feature on page 86, to assemble and quilt the curtain rows. Layer the tallest patchwork row (that uses the F strips) with its corresponding lining fabric and quilt. Then add the two shorter rows (with the E strips) and their lining pieces.

2 **Hem the edges.** Fold over the short side edges by ½" (1.5cm) to the back and iron the folds in place. Repeat with the long top and bottom edges. Fold over the side edges again, this time by ¾" (2cm). Repeat with the long top and bottom edges.

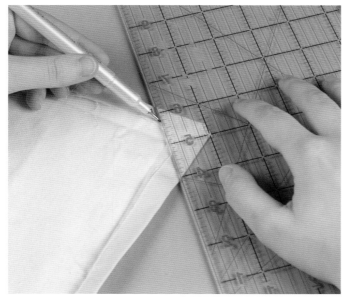

3 **Miter the corners.** Unfold the ¾" (2cm) folds and draw a diagonal line going across each corner where the creases meet. The 45° line on your ruler helps with this.

4 **Sew the corners.** Fold the curtain in half diagonally at one corner (right sides facing) so the two ends of the line meet. Sew along the line, then trim away the excess fabric to finish the mitered corner. Repeat with the remaining corners.

5 **Sew the curtain ties.** Fold a curtain tie piece in half lengthwise with right sides together. Sew along the edges of the rectangle, leaving a large 4" (10cm) opening in the raw long edge. Trim the seam allowances, turn the tie right side out, fold under the seam allowances around the opening, and press flat. Repeat with the remaining curtain ties.

6 **Finish the ties.** Edge stitch around the perimeter of each curtain tie to close up the opening for turning.

7 **Attach the ties.** Fold over the short side edges of the curtain by ¾" (2cm) to the back. Repeat with the long top and bottom edges. Fold the curtain ties in half widthwise and pin them at even intervals along the top edge of the curtain, aligning the fold of each tie with the fold of the curtain. Sew around the folded edge of the curtain, stitching the ties in place.

QUILT IT!

If you enjoyed making the offset squares block for the curtain project, try using it to make a quilt. Use the chart on page 121 to cut the pieces and assemble the blocks to form your quilt top. Then refer to the basic quilting guide on page 64 for information on how to finish the whole quilt.

• • • • • • • • • • • •

MINI-LESSON: SELF-BINDING

Like bagging out a quilt (page 73), self-binding is another way to finish a quilt without traditional binding. You can still achieve the same clean, mitered-corner edge, but without having to cut brand new binding fabric. For this method, make sure you have plenty of backing fabric so you don't shave things too close. The steps here are for ½" (1.5cm)-wide binding.

. . . .

1 Trim the batting and backing. Once all of the layers are quilted, trim the batting so it is flush with your quilt top, but allow the backing to extend 1" (2.5cm) beyond the edges of your quilt top and batting.

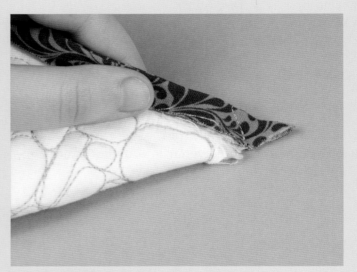

2 Miter the corners. Fold the backing over toward the front of the quilt along all edges twice, folding by ½" (1.5cm) both times (similar to Steps 2–4 of the curtain). Unfold the second set of folds and mark each corner at a 45° angle where the creases meet. Fold the quilt diagonally with right sides together at a corner so the ends of the line meet, and sew across the line. Repeat with the remaining corners.

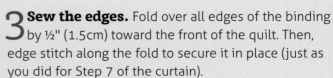

3 Sew the edges. Fold over all edges of the binding by ½" (1.5cm) toward the front of the quilt. Then, edge stitch along the fold to secure it in place (just as you did for Step 7 of the curtain).

TECHNIQUE:

Binding

After the layers of your quilt are all quilted, you can finally move on to the last step—binding! The most straightforward method of cleaning up those raw edges is to wrap them in a strip of fabric, not only to add extra strength, but as a design opportunity as well. You can choose a matching color of fabric so the edge of the quilt looks seamless, or use a contrasting fabric to make the border pop nicely.

BINDING ANATOMY

The strongest and easiest binding to work with is called double fold binding or French fold binding. This is made from a strip of fabric folded in half lengthwise (with wrong sides together), so one side of the strip has raw edges and the other side has a fold.

Binding that's cut along the crosswise grain (width) of your fabric is generally considered the best choice, because when it does eventually wear out and start to fray, the threads will deteriorate in a centralized location that's easy to repair rather than in a run that goes down your quilt.

The binding is attached by sewing both raw edges to the edge of the quilt, then wrapping it around the edge of the quilt and sewing the folded edge in place on the other side of the quilt.

CALCULATING HOW MUCH MATERIAL YOU NEED

A ⅜" (1cm)-wide finished binding is a good, happy medium—and it's what I've used for all the projects in this book—though you'll find a lot of seasoned quilters go with a ¼" (6mm) binding.

1. Take the width of the binding you want to make and multiply that by three to account for the three times the binding will cover the quilt edge. So for a ⅜" (1cm) binding: ⅜" x 3 = 1⅛" (1cm x 3 = 3cm).

2. Add ¼" (6mm) to account for the extra fabric needed to wrap the binding (1⅛" + ¼" = 1⅜" [3cm + 0.6cm = 3.6cm]).

3. Then multiply the sum by 2 to account for the double fold (1⅜" x 2 = 2¾") [3.6cm x 2 = 7.2cm]. This will be the width of the strip you'll need for your binding.

Here's the formula to use to find out how much quilting cotton you'll need for your binding:

1. Calculate the perimeter of your quilt (length + width x 2 = ___)

2. Add an extra 15" (38cm) for working room (X + 15"= ___ [X + 38cm = ___])

3. Divide that figure by 40" (101.5cm) as follows (X/40 = ___ [X/101.5 = ___])

4. Round up the answer to the nearest whole number.

5. Multiply that answer by your binding width. In this example, the binding width is 2¾" (7.2cm) like this (X x 2¾" = ___ [X x 7.2cm = ___])

6. Divide the answer by 36" (100cm) to get the number of yards (meters) this way (X/36 = ___ [X/100cm = ___])

7. Round up that figure to the nearest yardage cut—¼, ⅓, ½, ⅔, or ¾ yd. (for metric, round up to the next tenth of a meter)—to give yourself a bit of insurance.

SEWING

This is the basic and reliable method of mitered binding that most quilters use. Start by cutting the strips from your binding fabric in the width you calculated on page 95.

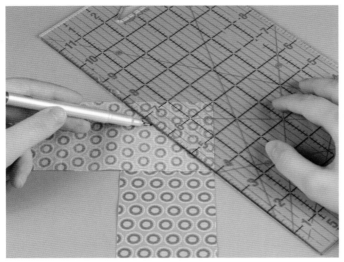

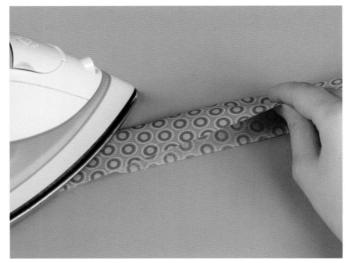

1 Chain your strips. To chain a long strip of binding, align the short ends of two pieces together at a right angle. Then, on the top piece, draw a diagonal line going from outside corner to outside corner. This will be your seam line. The inside corner is never used in a diagonal seam. Sew all your strips together, one after the next, this way.

2 Fold the strip. After pressing the diagonal seam allowances open, fold the entire strip in half lengthwise with wrong sides together. Iron the entire strip flat to be ready to sew.

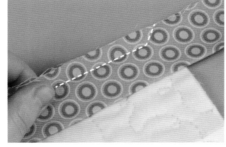

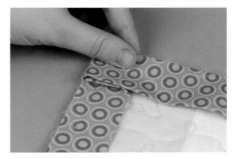

3 Begin the binding. Start attaching your binding along the middle of one side of your quilt as follows. Align the raw edge of the binding along the right side of the quilt and, leaving about 6" (15cm) of the end of your binding unattached, sew using a seam allowance equal to the (finished) binding width. Before you approach the corner, refer to the next step!

4 Sew the corner. When you are ⅜" (1cm) away (or a distance equal to your binding width) from the next edge, stop sewing, pivot the quilt, and sew off the edge at a diagonal toward the corner of the quilt.

5 Fold the corner. To create the mitered edge corner, fold your binding to the side and away from the quilt against the diagonally stitched line. Then fold it back down over itself, aligning the long edge with the next side of the quilt, creating a little triangle fold in the corner.

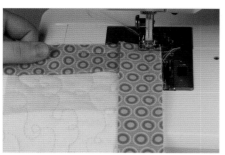

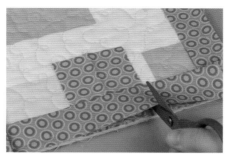

6 Finish the corner. To complete the corner, begin stitching the next side of the quilt, sewing over the folds of the miter with plenty of backstitches so the corner is very strong. Then continue stitching the remainder of the binding to the edges of the quilt, mitering at each corner. As you approach your starting point, refer to the next step.

7 Overlap the ends. Stop sewing about 12" (30.5cm) short of your starting point. Overlap the starting and finishing ends of your binding on the edge of your quilt. Trim off a bit of extra binding, unfold it, and place it above the overlap (this scrap will serve as a guide). On both sides of the scrap, trim any excess binding that extends beyond its width.

8 Join the ends. Unfold and bring together the starting and finishing ends of the binding with right sides facing. Sew them on the diagonal just as in Step 1. Trim the seam allowance, press the seam open, and fold the binding back up lengthwise. Align the unattached binding with the corresponding edge of the quilt and stitch it in place. The binding is now attached completely around the front of the quilt.

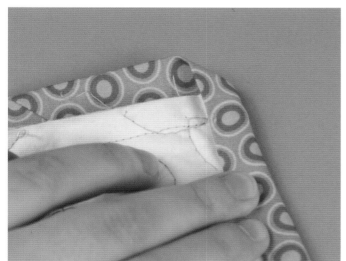

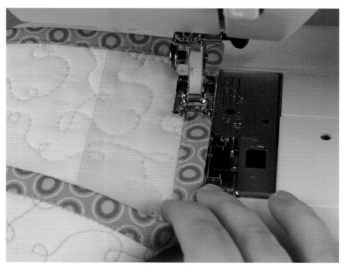

9 Wrap the binding. Press the binding away from the quilt, then wrap it around the edge to the back. For the corners, you'll need to fold one side at a time, overlapping the folds as if you were wrapping a package. The folded edge should extend a little beyond the previous seam. Pin and iron the folded binding in place.

10 Attach the binding. While traditionalists sew this part by hand, a faster option is to sew around the front of the quilt using a narrow zigzag stitch centered over the previous seam. This should catch the edge of your binding that's folded to the back, anchoring it in place. Check the back of your quilt occasionally to make sure this is happening.

Basket Weave Potholder

Put all of your newfound skills together into this easy and classic potholder project! The insulated batting inside means every potholder is really just like a mini-quilt, complete with patchwork, quilting, and binding. Once you've mastered this, not only will you have a thoroughly modern kitchen accent, you'll have all the skills you need to tackle a full-size quilt.

MATERIALS

FABRIC

4 different focus fabrics: ⅛ yd. (0.2m) each

Background fabric: ⅛ yd. (0.2m)

Lining fabric: ¼ yd. (0.3m)

Binding fabric: ⅛ yd. (0.2m)

OTHER MATERIALS

Thin cotton batting: ¼ yd. (0.3m)

Insulated batting: 9" x 9" (22.9 x 22.9cm)

DIFFICULTY: ⬡ ⬡ ⬡

MAKES:
One 6½" x 6½" (16.5 x 16.5cm) pot holder

TECHNIQUES:
Rotary cutting (page 24)
Piecing (page 28)
Machine quilting (page 74)
Binding (page 95)

SUGGESTED FABRICS:
Quilting cotton, 100% linen, 100% cotton flannel

TOOLS
Quilter's toolkit (see page 13)

CUTTING PLAN

Gather the patchwork fabrics and, following the rotary cutting instructions on page 24, cut the following fabric strips along the width of the fabric yardage. Then subcut the strips as directed below. Sort the pieces into the lettered units, labeling them with sticky notes if desired. After the patchwork pieces have been cut, cut the indicated pieces from the lining fabric, batting, and binding. Feel free to use a rotary cutter for speed and ease.

From Color 1 cut:

1 strip: 1½" (3.8cm) x width of fabric; subcut into:

- **1 square:** 1½" x 1½" (3.8 x 3.8cm) (A)

- **1 rectangle:** 1½" x 3½" (3.8 x 8.9cm) (B)

From Color 2 cut:

1 strip: 1½" (3.8cm) x width of fabric; subcut into:

- **2 squares:** 1½" x 1½" (3.8 x 3.8cm) (C)

- **1 rectangle:** 1½" x 3½" (3.8 x 8.9cm) (D)

From Color 3 cut:

1 strip: 2½" (6.4cm) x width of fabric; subcut into:

- **1 rectangle:** 1½" x 2½" (3.8 x 6.4cm) (E)

- **1 rectangle:** 2½" x 4½" (6.4 x 11.4cm) (F)

From Color 4 cut:

1 strip: 2½" (6.4cm) x width of fabric; subcut into:

- **1 rectangle:** 1½" x 2½" (3.8 x 6.4cm) (G)

- **1 rectangle:** 2½" x 3½" (6.4 x 8.9cm) (H)

From the background fabric cut:

1 strip: 1½" (3.8cm) x width of fabric; subcut into:

- **9 squares:** 1½" x 1½" (3.8 x 3.8cm) (I)

From the lining fabric cut:

1 square: 9" x 9" (22.9 x 22.9cm) (Potholder back)
1 rectangle: 8" x 6½" (20.3 x 16.5cm) (Potholder pocket)

From the cotton batting cut:

1 square: 9" x 9" (22.9 x 22.9cm) (Backing)
1 rectangle: 6½" x 4 (16.5 x 10.2cm) (Pocket)
If you have not already done so, cut a 9" x 9" (22.9 x 22.9cm) square from the insulated batting (Insulation)

From the binding fabric cut:

1 strip: 2¾" x 40" (7cm x 101.6cm) (Binding)

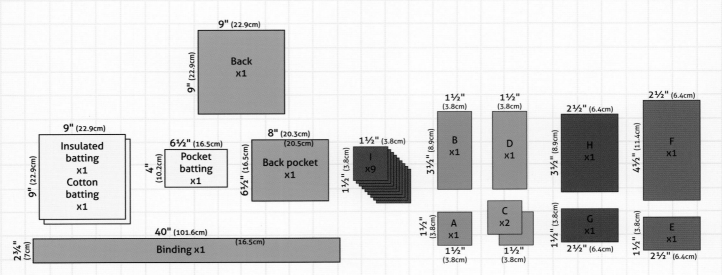

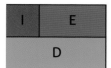

Figure A.

Figure B.

Figure C.

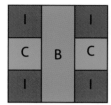

Figure D.

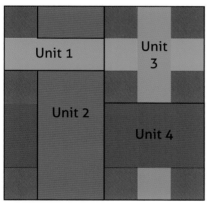

Figure E.

PIECING

Set aside the cut lining, batting, and binding pieces for now. Gather all the patchwork pieces for piecing. All seam allowances are a scant ¼" (6mm). Press the seam allowances open or to the side as you prefer; mine are pressed open.

1. The basket weave block is made by stitching together four square units to make a larger square. For Unit 1, sew an I square to one short edge of an E rectangle. Then, add a D rectangle to the bottom long edge of the pieced strip (Figure A).

2. For Unit 2, sew an I square to each short edge of a G rectangle. Then, add an F rectangle to the right long edge of the pieced strip (Figure B).

3. For Unit 3, sew an I square to two opposing edges of a C square. Repeat this once more to create a second I/C/I strip. Sew one I/C/I strip to each long edge of a B rectangle (Figure C).

4. For Unit 4, sew an I square to two opposing edges of an A square. Then, add an H rectangle to the top long edge of the pieced strip (Figure D).

5. Sew Units 1 and 2 into a column, matching up the like colors. Then sew Units 3 and 4 into a column. Join the two columns, matching up the like colors, to finish the basket weave block. It should measure 6½" x 6½" (16.5 x 16.5cm) (Figure E).

ASSEMBLY

A ⅜" (1cm) seam allowance is used for attaching the binding.

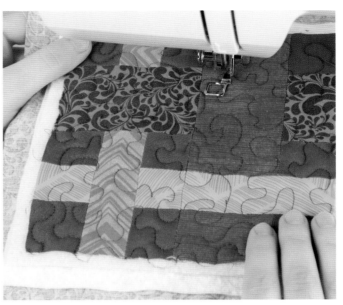

1 Layer the potholder fabrics. Layer the pieces of your quilt sandwich as follows: lining fabric (wrong side up), cotton batting, insulated batting, patchwork (right side up). Baste the layers together with a few safety pins or sewing pins as desired.

2 Quilt the layers. Following the machine quilting feature (page 74), machine quilt a pattern through all the layers of fabric and batting. When complete, trim off the excess batting and backing material.

3 Form the pocket. Fold the pocket piece in half widthwise (bringing the short ends together) with wrong sides facing. Slip the cotton batting between the layers, placing one long edge of the batting against the inside of the fold in the pocket. Anchor the batting by edge stitching along the top folded edge of the pocket.

4 Baste the pocket. With both pieces right side up, place the pocket on top of the back of the potholder, aligning the raw bottom edges. Baste the pocket in place along the sides and bottom.

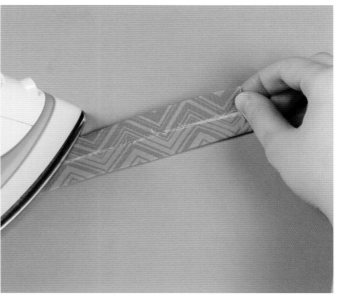

5 Add the binding. Following the binding feature (page 95), prepare the binding from your binding fabric. Trim off 6" (16.5cm) and set it aside. Apply the rest of the binding fabric around the perimeter of your potholder following the steps on pages 96–97, but stop before you reach Step 9, where the binding is wrapped.

6 Create the loop. Use the 6" (16.5cm) of leftover binding fabric to create a loop. Fold the long raw edges of the strip in to meet at the center fold. Iron these folds in place. Fold the strip along the center fold, then edge stitch along the open long edge to create a finished strip.

7 Attach the loop. Fold the strip in half widthwise to form a loop. Center the raw short ends on the back of the potholder on the side opposite the pocket. Baste the loop in place along the edge of the potholder, making sure not to sew the binding.

8 Flip the loop. Starting with Step 9 on page 97, complete the last steps of the binding technique, wrapping the binding over the end of the loop and sewing it in place. When complete, fold the loop back on itself so it extends past the top edge of the potholder. Stitch it in place with a few slip stitches.

QUILT IT!

If you liked the basket weave block used for the potholder project, try making a full quilt from it! Use the chart on page 123 to cut the pieces and assemble the blocks to form your quilt top. Then refer to the basic quilting guide on page 64 for information on how to finish the whole quilt.

• • • • • • • • • • • •

TRADITIONAL TWIST

This project can be done with any quilt block that catches your eye. A traditional block is used here for a comforting look that still has some bold geometry. This block is a slight variation of the Friendship Star.

• •

FABRIC

White background fabric: ⅛ yd. (0.2m)

Blue focus fabric: ⅛ yd. (0.2cm)

Yellow focus fabric: ⅛ yd. (0.2cm)

Lining fabric: ¼ yd. (0.3m)

Binding fabric: ⅛ yd. (0.2m)

OTHER MATERIALS

Thin cotton batting: ¼ yd. (0.3m)

Insulated batting: 9" x 9" (22.9 x 22.9cm) square

TOOLS

Quilter's toolkit (see page 13)

CUTTING PLAN

From the white background fabric cut:
1 square: 2½" x 2½" (6.4 x 6.4cm) (A)
1 strip: 2⅞" (7.3cm) x width of fabric; subcut into:
• **4 squares:** 2⅞" x 2⅞" (7.3 x 7.3cm) (B)

From the blue focus fabric cut:
1 strip: 2⅞" (7.3cm) x width of fabric; subcut into:
• **2 squares:** 2⅞" x 2⅞" (7.3 x 7.3cm) (C)

From the yellow focus fabric cut:
1 strip: 2⅞" (7.3cm) x width of fabric; subcut into:
• **2 squares:** 2⅞" x 2⅞" (7.3 x 7.3cm) (D)

From the lining fabric cut:
1 square: 9" x 9" (22.9 x 22.9cm) (Potholder back)
1 rectangle: 8" x 6½" (20.3 x 16.5cm)
    (Potholder pocket)

From the cotton batting cut:
1 square: 9" x 9" (22.9 x 22.9cm) (Backing)
1 rectangle: 6½" x 4 (16.5 x 10.2cm) (Pocket)
If you have not already done so, cut a 9" x 9" (22.9 x 22.9cm) square from the insulated batting (Insulation)

From the binding fabric cut:
1 strip: 2¾" x 40" (7cm x 101.6cm) (Binding)

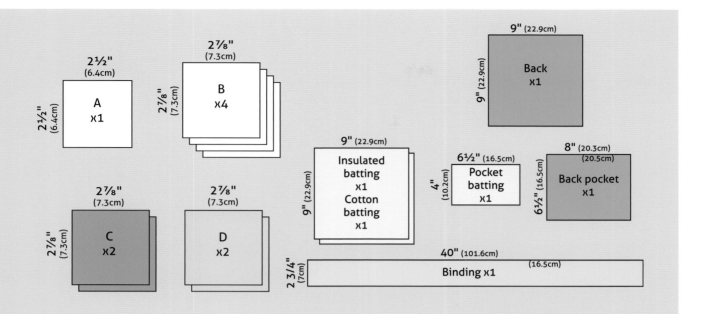

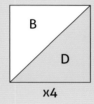

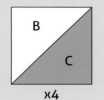

Figure A.

Figure B.

PIECING

1. Following the triangle piecing feature (page 56), create: four half-square triangle units of blue and white squares (B & C) and four half-square triangle units of yellow and white squares (B & D) (Figure A).

2. Arrange the squares in the configuration shown in Figure B.

3. Sew the squares together into rows; then join the rows to create the finished block. Be sure to lock your seams (if each row's seam allowances were pressed to the side) or match up the seam lines (if the seam allowances were pressed open).

4. When finished, the block should measure 6½" x 6½" (16.5 x 16.5cm)

ASSEMBLY

Follow the assembly instructions on pages 102–103 to complete the potholder. This traditional quilt block replaces the original 6½" x 6½" (16.5 x 16.5cm) basketweave quilt block featured in the project.

Quilt It!

Now that you've learned all the necessary skills to make a quilt and have had the chance to practice on some small projects, you might be itching to dive into your first full-size quilt project. If you're ready to take the next step, you'll be happy to know that all the info you need is right here at your fingertips. In this chapter, you will find a materials list and cutting plan for creating a full-size quilt from any of the blocks used in this book. Simply follow the chart for the block of your choice to gather and cut the pieces. Then, follow the assembly instructions from the practice project in the book to assemble the blocks and create your quilt top!

STYLISH STRIPS PILLOW COVER QUILT

Use the following chart to cut the pieces and assemble the blocks to form your quilt top. Then refer to the basic quilting guide on page 64 for the steps needed to finish. Note that, for simplicity, all the (E) strips have been replaced with (D) strips, so every background strip is the same for each block. Try out a warm color scheme such as the one in the photo on page 32 for a brighter look, or check out the illustrations below for some additional color variations.

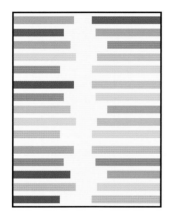
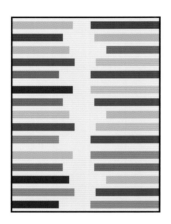
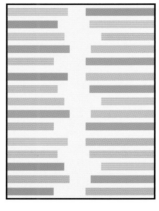

Color variations. Would you like to make this quilt in a different color palette? Check out the options here to spark your creativity.

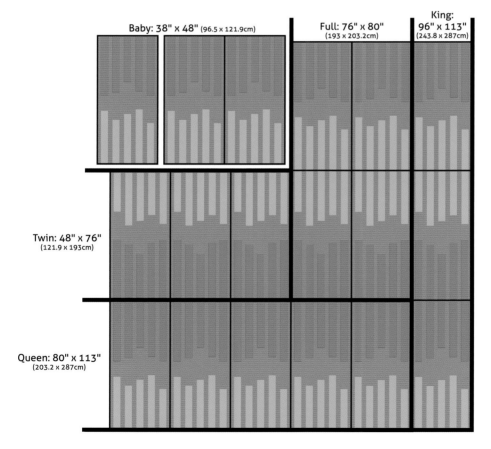

Baby: 38" x 48" (96.5 x 121.9cm)

Full: 76" x 80" (193 x 203.2cm)

King: 96" x 113" (243.8 x 287cm)

Twin: 48" x 76" (121.9 x 193cm)

Queen: 80" x 113" (203.2 x 287cm)

Quilt layout. Use the number of blocks indicated by the illustration and the chart to construct your quilt to size.

	Baby	Twin	Full	Queen	King
Finished size	38" x 48" (96.5 x 121.9cm)	48" x 76" (121.9 x 193cm)	76" x 80" (193 x 203.2cm)	80" x 113" (203.2 x 287cm)	96" x 113" (243.8 x 287cm)
Block configuration	1 block x 3 blocks (3 total)	2 blocks x 3 blocks (6 total)	2 blocks x 5 blocks (10 total)	5 blocks x 3 blocks (15 total)	6 blocks x 3 blocks (18 total)
Materials Needed					
Background fabric	1¼ yd. (1.2m)	2¼ yd. (2.1m)	3⅓ yd. (3.1m)	5 yd. (4.6m)	6 yd. (5.5m)
Various green prints	⅔ yd. (0.6m)	1¼ yd. (1.2m)	2 yd. (1.9m)	2¾ yd. (2.6m)	3¼ yd. (3m)
Various blue prints	⅔ yd. (0.6m)	1¼ yd. (1.2m)	2 yd. (1.9m)	2¾ yd. (2.6m)	3¼ yd. (3m)
Batting	46" x 56" (116.8 x 142.2cm)	56" x 84" (142.2 x 213.3cm)	84" x 88" (213.3 x 223.5cm)	88" x 121" (223.5 x 307.3cm)	104" x 121" (264.1 x 307.3cm)
Backing	1¾ yd. (1.7m) of 60" (152.4cm)-wide backing	1¾ yd. (1.7m) of 106" (269.2cm)-wide backing	2½ yd. (2.3m) of 106" (269.2cm)-wide backing	3½ yd. (3.2m) of 106" (269.2cm)-wide backing	3½ yd. (3.2m) of 118" (299.7cm)-wide backing
⅜" (1cm)-wide binding	½ yd. (0.5m)	⅔ yd. (0.6m)	¾ yd. (0.7m)	1 yd. (1m)	1 yd. (1m)
Blue fabric					
Strips to cut:	8 strips: 2½" (6.4cm) x width of fabric	15 strips: 2½" (6.4cm) x width of fabric	25 strips: 2½" (6.4cm) x width of fabric	38 strips: 2½" (6.4cm) x width of fabric	45 strips: 2½" (6.4cm) x width of fabric
Subcut into:	15 strips: 2½" x 20" (A) [6.4 x 50.8cm]	30 strips: 2½" x 20" (A) [6.4 x 50.8cm]	50 strips: 2½" x 20" (A) [6.4 x 50.8cm]	75 strips: 2½" x 20" (A) [6.4 x 50.8cm]	90 strips: 2½" x 20" (A) [6.4 x 50.8cm]
Green fabric					
Strips to cut:	8 strips: 2½" (6.4cm) x width of fabric	15 strips: 2½" (6.4cm) x width of fabric	25 strips: 2½" (6.4cm) x width of fabric	38 strips: 2½" (6.4cm) x width of fabric	45 strips: 2½" (6.4cm) x width of fabric
Subcut into:	15 strips: 2½" x 20" (B) [6.4 x 50.8cm]	30 strips: 2½" x 20" (B) [6.4 x 50.8cm]	50 strips: 2½" x 20" (B) [6.4 x 50.8cm]	75 strips: 2½" x 20" (B) [6.4 x 50.8cm]	90 strips: 2½" x 20" (B) [6.4 x 50.8cm]
Background fabric					
Strips to cut:	3 strips: 2½" (6.4cm) x width of fabric	6 strips: 2½" (6.4cm) x width of fabric	10 strips: 2½" (6.4cm) x width of fabric	15 strips: 2½" (6.4cm) x width of fabric	18 strips: 2½" (6.4cm) x width of fabric
Subcut into:	15 random rectangles between 3"–7" [7.6–17.8cm] (C)	30 random rectangles between 3"–7" [7.6–17.8cm] (C)	50 random rectangles between 3"–7" [7.6–17.8cm] (C)	75 random rectangles between 3"–7" [7.6–17.8cm] (C)	90 random rectangles between 3"–7" [7.6–17.8cm] (C)
Strips to cut:	18 strips: 1½" (3.8cm) x width of fabric (D)	36 strips: 1½" (3.8cm) x width of fabric (D)	60 strips: 1½" (3.8cm) x width of fabric (D)	90 strips: 1½" (3.8cm) x width of fabric (D)	108 strips: 1½" (3.8cm) x width of fabric (D)
Trim each strip to:	38" (96.5cm) long	38" (96.5cm) long	38" (96.5cm) long	38" (96.5cm) long	38" (96.5cm) long

PRECUT PERFECT!

The focus fabrics can also be replaced by one roll of 2½" (6.4cm)-wide precut strips, such as jelly rolls. For the full-size quilts here, you'll need the following number of precut strips: 16 (baby), 30 (twin), 50 (full), 76 (queen), and 90 (king).

BEDSIDE ORGANIZER QUILT

Use the following chart to cut the pieces and assemble the blocks to form your quilt top. Then refer to the basic quilting guide on page 64 for the steps needed to finish. Because the block is so small, I added some thick borders around the edges to create a very light and modern effect across the entire quilt. Simply follow the chart to cut the extra rectangles needed to add these borders to your finished blocks.

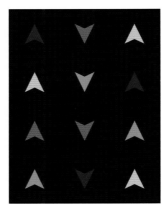

Color variations. Would you like to make this quilt in a different color palette? Check out the options here to spark your creativity.

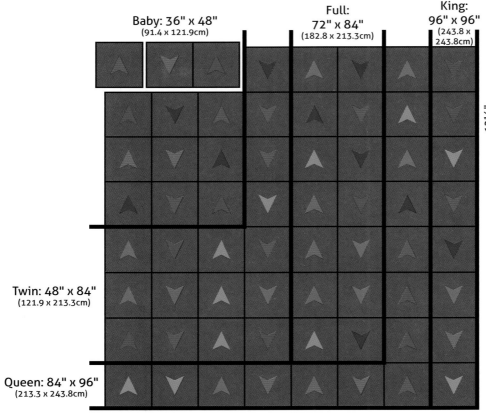

Baby: 36" x 48"
(91.4 x 121.9cm)

Full:
72" x 84"
(182.8 x 213.3cm)

King:
96" x 96"
(243.8 x 243.8cm)

Twin: 48" x 84"
(121.9 x 213.3cm)

Queen: 84" x 96"
(213.3 x 243.8cm)

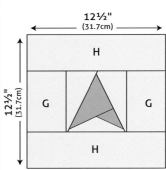

12½"
(31.7cm)

12½"
(31.7cm)

H

G   G

H

Block layout. Add two (G) rectangles to each side, then two (H) rectangles to the top and bottom of your foundation piecing to create a consistent 12½" x 12½" (32 x 32cm) block for your quilt.

Quilt layout. Use the number of blocks indicated by the illustration and the chart to construct your quilt to size.

	Baby	Twin	Full	Queen	King
Finished size	36" x 48" (91.4 x 121.9cm)	48" x 84" (121.9 x 213.3cm)	72" x 84" (182.8 x 213.3cm)	84" x 96" (213.3 x 243.8cm)	96" x 96" (243.8 x 243.8cm)
Block configuration	3 blocks x 4 blocks (12 total)	4 blocks x 7 blocks (28 total)	6 blocks x 7 blocks (42 total)	7 blocks x 8 blocks (56 total)	8 blocks x 8 blocks (64 total)
Materials Needed					
Focus fabrics, totaling:	⅔ yd. (0.6m)	1 yd. (1m)	1½ yd. (1.4m)	1¾ yd. (1.7m)	2 yd. (1.9m)
Background fabric	2¼ yd. (2.1m)	4⅔ yd. (4.3m)	6¾" yd. (6.2m)	9¼ yd. (8.5m)	10¼" yd. (9.4m)
Batting	44" x 56" (111.7 x 142.2cm)	56" x 92" (142.2 x 233.6cm)	80" x 92" (203.2 x 233.6cm)	92" x 104" (233.6 x 264.1cm)	104" x 104" (264.1 x 264.1cm)
Backing	1⅔ yd. (1.6m) of 60" (152.4cm)-wide backing	1⅔ yd. (1.6m) of 106" (269.2cm)-wide backing	2⅓ yd. (2.2m) of 106" (269.2cm)-wide backing	2¾ (2.6m) yd. of 118" (299.7cm)-wide backing	3 yd. (2.8m) of 118" (299.7cm)-wide backing
Binding	½ yd. (0.5m)	⅔ yd. (0.6m)	¾ yd. (0.7m)	1 yd. (1m)	1 yd. (1m)
Focus fabric					
Strips to cut:	2 strips: 3" (7.6cm) x width of fabric	3 strips: 3" (7.6cm) x width of fabric	5 strips: 3" (7.6cm) x width of fabric	6 strips: 3" (7.6cm) x width of fabric	7 strips: 3" (7.6cm) x width of fabric
Subcut into:	12 rectangles: 4" x 3" (A) (10.2 x 7.6)	28 rectangles: 4" x 3" (A) (10.2 x 7.6)	42 rectangles: 4" x 3" (A) (10.2 x 7.6)	56 rectangles: 4" x 3" (A) (10.2 x 7.6)	64 rectangles: 4" x 3" (A) (10.2 x 7.6)
Strips to cut:	2 strips: 6" (15.2cm) x width of fabric	4 strips: 6" (15.2cm) x width of fabric	6 strips: 6" (15.2cm) x width of fabric	7 strips: 6" (15.2cm) x width of fabric	8 strips: 6" (15.2cm) x width of fabric
Subcut into:	12 rectangles: 5" x 6" (C) (12.7 x 15.2cm)	28 rectangles: 5" x 6" (C) (12.7 x 15.2cm)	42 rectangles: 5" x 6" (C) (12.7 x 15.2cm)	56 rectangles: 5" x 6" (C) (12.7 x 15.2cm)	64 rectangles: 5" x 6" (C) (12.7 x 15.2cm)
Background fabric					
Strips to cut:	7 strips: 4" (10.2cm) x width of fabric	15 strips: 4" (10.2cm) x width of fabric	23 strips: 4" (10.2cm) x width of fabric	30 strips: 4" (10.2cm) x width of fabric	34 strips: 4" (10.2cm) x width of fabric
Subcut into:	12 rectangles: 4" x 6" (B) (10.2 x 15.2cm)	28 rectangles: 4" x 6" (B) (10.2 x 15.2cm)	42 rectangles: 4" x 6" (B) (10.2 x 15.2cm)	56 rectangles: 4" x 6" (B) (10.2 x 15.2cm)	64 rectangles: 4" x 6" (B) (10.2 x 15.2cm)
	12 rectangles: 4" x 7" (D) (10.2 x 17.8cm)	28 rectangles: 4" x 7" (D) (10.2 x 17.8cm)	42 rectangles: 4" x 7" (D) (10.2 x 17.8cm)	56 rectangles: 4" x 7" (D) (10.2 x 17.8cm)	64 rectangles: 4" x 7" (D) (10.2 x 17.8cm)
	12 rectangles: 4" x 8" (E) (10.2 x 20.3cm)	28 rectangles: 4" x 8" (E) (10.2 x 20.3cm)	42 rectangles: 4" x 8" (E) (10.2 x 20.3cm)	56 rectangles: 4" x 8" (E) (10.2 x 20.3cm)	64 rectangles: 4" x 8" (E) (10.2 x 20.3cm)
Strips to cut:	3 strips: 6" (15.2cm) x width of fabric	6 strips: 6" (15.2cm) x width of fabric	9 strips: 6" (15.2cm) x width of fabric	12 strips: 6" (15.2cm) x width of fabric	13 strips: 6" (15.2cm) x width of fabric
Subcut into:	24 rectangles: 3⅞" x 6" (G) (9.8 x 15.2cm)	56 rectangles: 3⅞" x 6" (G) (9.8 x 15.2cm)	84 rectangles: 3⅞" x 6" (G) (9.8 x 15.2cm)	112 rectangles: 3⅞" x 6" (G) (9.8 x 15.2cm)	128 rectangles: 3⅞" x 6" (G) (9.8 x 15.2cm)
Strips to cut:	8 strips: 3¾" (9.5cm) x width of fabric	19 strips: 3¾" (9.5cm) x width of fabric	28 strips: 3¾" (9.5cm) x width of fabric	38 strips: 3¾" (9.5cm) x width of fabric	43 strips: 3¾" (9.5cm) x width of fabric
Subcut into:	24 rectangles: 12½" x 3¾" (H) (31.8 x 9.5cm)	56 rectangles: 12½" x 3¾" (H) (31.8 x 9.5cm)	84 rectangles: 12½" x 3¾" (H) (31.8 x 9.5cm)	112 rectangles: 12½" x 3¾" (H) (31.8 x 9.5cm)	128 rectangles: 12½" x 3¾" (H) (31.8 x 9.5cm)

PRECUT PERFECT!

A 10" x 10" (25.5 x 25.5cm) charm pack can easily be used for the focus fabrics in this project. For the full-size quilts here, you'll need the following number of charm squares: 12 (baby), 28 (twin), 42 (full), 56 (queen), and 64 (king).

NESTING FABRIC BOXES QUILT

Use the following chart to cut the pieces and assemble the blocks to form your quilt top. Then refer to the basic quilting guide on page 64 for the steps needed to finish. This quilt uses the block made for the large box on page 48.

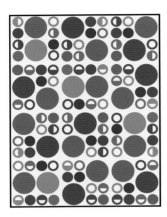
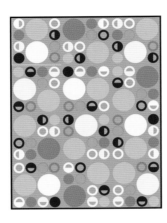
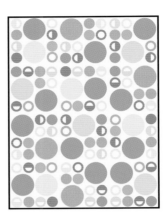

Color variations. Would you like to make this quilt in a different color palette? Check out the options here to spark your creativity.

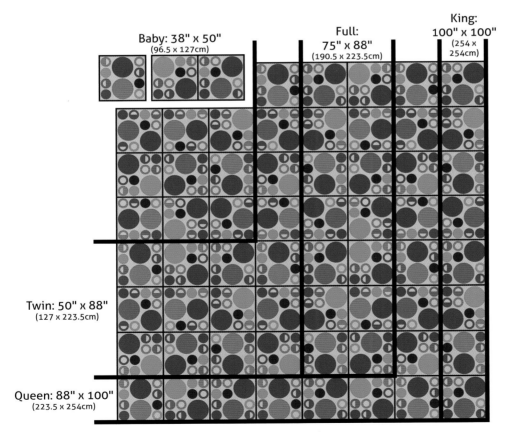

Baby: 38" x 50"
(96.5 x 127cm)

Full:
75" x 88"
(190.5 x 223.5cm)

King:
100" x 100"
(254 x 254cm)

Twin: 50" x 88"
(127 x 223.5cm)

Queen: 88" x 100"
(223.5 x 254cm)

Quilt layout. Use the number of blocks indicated by the illustration and the chart to construct your quilt to size.

	Baby	Twin	Full	Queen	King
Finished size	38 x 50" (96.5 x 127cm)	50" x 88" (127 x 223.5cm)	75" x 88" (190.5 x 223.5cm)	88" x 100" (223.5x 254cm)	100" x 100" (254 x 254cm)
Block configuration	3 blocks x 4 blocks (12 total)	4 blocks x 7 blocks (28 total)	6 blocks x 7 blocks (42 total)	7 blocks x 8 blocks (56 total)	8 blocks x 8 blocks (64 total)
Materials Needed					
Various focus fabrics, totaling:	1½ yd. (1.4m)	3½ yd. (3m)	5 yd. (4.6m)	6⅔ yd. (6.1m)	7½yd. (6.9m)
Background fabric	1½ yd. (1.4m)	3¾ yd. (3.4m)	5¼ yd. (4.9m)	7 yd. (6.5m)	8yd. (7.3m)
20" (50.8)-wide fusible web	1¼ yd. (1.2m)	2¾ yd. (2.6m)	4 yd. (3.7m)	5½ yd. (5m)	6¼ yd. (5.8m)
Batting	46" x 58" (116.8 x 147.3cm)	58" x 96" (147.3 x 243.8cm)	83" x 96" (210.8 x 243.8cm)	96" x 108" (243.8 x 274.3cm)	108" x 108" (274.3 x 274.3cm)
Backing	1¾ yd. (1.7m) of 60" (152.4cm)-wide backing	1¾ yd. (1.7m) of 106" (269.2cm)-wide backing	2½ yd. (2.3m) of 106" (269.2cm)-wide backing	2¾ yd. (2.6m) of 118" (299.7cm)-wide backing	3¼ yd. (3m) of 118" (299.7m)-wide backing
Binding	½ yd. (0.5m)	⅔ yd. (0.6m)	¾ yd. (0.7m)	1 yd. (1m)	1 yd. (1m)
Background fabric					
Strips to cut:	4 strips: 13" (33cm) x width of fabric	10 strips: 13" (33cm) x width of fabric	14 strips: 13" (33cm) x width of fabric	19 strips: 13" (33cm) x width of fabric	22 strips: 13" (33cm) x width of fabric
Subcut into:	12 squares: 13" x 13" (33 x 33cm)	28 squares: 13" x 13" (33 x 33cm)	42 squares: 13" x 13" (33 x 33cm)	56 squares: 13" x 13" (33 x 33cm)	64 squares: 13" x 13" (33 x 33cm)
Appliqué pieces					
Pieces to cut:	Assortment of 24 large circles	Assortment of 56 large circles	Assortment of 84 large circles	Assortment of 112 large circles	Assortment of 128 large circles
	Assortment of 96 small circles	Assortment of 224 small circles	Assortment of 336 small circles	Assortment of 448 small circles	Assortment of 512 small circles

PRECUT PERFECT!

A 10" x 10" (25.5 x 25.5cm) charm pack is perfect for the focus fabrics in this project. The charm squares are big enough to fit the large circles and will guarantee an assortment of small circles as well. For the full-size quilts here, you'll need at least the following number of charm squares: 24 (baby), 56 (twin), 84 (full), 112 (queen), and 128 (king).

CHEVRON TABLET COVER QUILT

Use the following chart to cut the pieces and assemble the blocks to form your quilt top. Then refer to the basic quilting guide on page 64 for the steps needed to finish. For seamless tiling, use the same fabric for the bottom and top chevron—check out the diagram on page 115 to get a better idea of how the larger design would come together. For ease, the triangle units have been enlarged to 4" (10.2cm) squares to make the quilt top piecing much faster.

Color variations. Would you like to make this quilt in a different color palette? Check out the options here to spark your creativity.

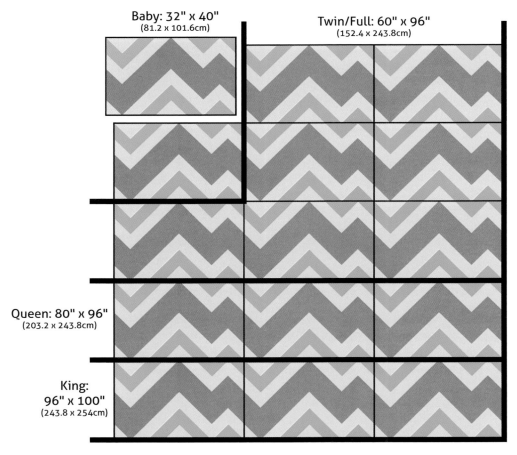

Baby: 32" x 40"
(81.2 x 101.6cm)

Twin/Full: 60" x 96"
(152.4 x 243.8cm)

Queen: 80" x 96"
(203.2 x 243.8cm)

King: 96" x 100"
(243.8 x 254cm)

Quilt layout. Use the number of blocks indicated by the illustration and the chart to construct your quilt to size.

	Baby	Full	Queen	King
Finished size	32" x 40" (81.2 x 101.6cm)	60" x 96" (152.4 x 243.8cm)	80" x 96" (203.2 x 243.8cm)	96" x 100" (243.8 x 254cm)
Block configuration	1 block x 2 blocks (2 total)	3 blocks x 3 blocks (9 total)	4 blocks x 3 blocks (12 total)	3 blocks x 5 blocks (15 total)
Materials Needed				
Small chevron fabric	⅓ yd. (0.4m)	1¼ yd. (1.2m)	1⅔ yd. (1.6m)	2¼ yd. (2.1m)
Large chevron fabric	⅔ yd. (0.6m)	2½ yd. (2.3m)	3¼ yd. (3m)	4 yd. (3.7m)
Background fabric	⅔ yd. (0.6m)	2½ yd. (2.3m)	3⅓ yd. (3.1m)	4¼ yd. (3.9m)
Batting	40" x 48" (101.6 x 121.9cm)	68" x 104" (172.7 x 264.1cm)	88" x 104" (223.5 x 264.1cm)	104" x 108" (264.1 x 274.3cm)
Backing	1¼ yd. (1.2m) of 60" (152.4cm)-wide backing	2 yd. (1.9m) of 118" (299.7cm)-wide backing	2⅔ yds. (2.5m) of 118" (299.7m)-wide backing	3 yd. (2.8m) of 118" (299.7cm)-wide backing
Binding	½ yd. (0.5m)	¾ yd. (0.7m)	1 yd. (1m)	1 yd. (1m)
Small chevron fabric				
Strips to cut:	2 strips: 4⅞" (12.4cm) x width of fabric	9 strips: 4⅞" (12.4cm) x width of fabric	12 strips: 4⅞" (12.4cm) x width of fabric	15 strips: 4⅞" (12.4cm) x width of fabric
Subcut into:	16 squares: 4⅞" x 4⅞" (A) (12.4 x 12.4cm)	72 squares: 4⅞" x 4⅞" (A) (12.4 x 12.4cm)	96 squares: 4⅞" x 4⅞" (A) (12.4 x 12.4cm)	120 squares: 4⅞" x 4⅞" (A) (12.4 x 12.4cm)
Large chevron fabric				
Strips to cut:	2 strips: 4⅞" (12.4cm) x width of fabric	9 strips: 4⅞" (12.4cm) x width of fabric	12 strips: 4⅞" (12.4cm) x width of fabric	15 strips: 4⅞" (12.4cm) x width of fabric
Subcut into:	16 squares: 4⅞" x 4⅞" (B) (12.4 x 12.4cm)	72 squares: 4⅞" x 4⅞" (B) (12.4 x 12.4cm)	96 squares: 4⅞" x 4⅞" (B) (12.4 x 12.4cm)	120 squares: 4⅞" x 4⅞" (B) (12.4 x 12.4cm)
Strips to cut:	2 strips: 4½" (11.4cm) x width of fabric	9 strips: 4½" (11.4cm) x width of fabric	12 strips: 4½" (11.4cm) x width of fabric	15 strips: 4½" (11.4cm) x width of fabric
Subcut into:	16 squares: 4½" x 4½" (C) (11.4 x 11.4cm)	72 squares: 4½" x 4½" (C) (11.4 x 11.4cm)	96 squares: 4½" x 4½" (C) (11.4 x 11.4cm)	120 squares: 4½" x 4½" (C) (11.4 x 11.4cm)
Background fabric				
Strips to cut:	4 strips: 4⅞" (12.4cm) x width of fabric	18 strips: 4⅞" (12.4cm) x width of fabric	24 strips: 4⅞" (12.4cm) x width of fabric	30 strips: 4⅞" (12.4cm) x width of fabric
Subcut into:	32 squares: 4⅞" x 4⅞" (E) (12.4 x 12.4cm)	144 squares: 4⅞" x 4⅞" (E) (12.4 x 12.4cm)	192 squares: 4⅞" x 4⅞" (E) (12.4 x 12.4cm)	240 squares: 4⅞" x 4⅞" (E) (12.4 x 12.4cm)

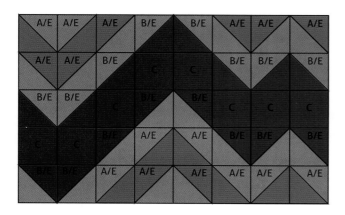

Block layout. Assemble the block units slightly differently than in the project instructions to get a perfectly tiling chevron.

BRAIDED SCARF QUILT

Use the following chart to cut the pieces and assemble the blocks to form your quilt top. Then refer to the basic quilting guide on page 64 for the steps needed to finish. For these quilts, horizontal sashing strips are used between the braids to give them the fresh and modern look that extra negative space achieves.

Color variations. Would you like to make this quilt in a different color palette? Check out the options here to spark your creativity.

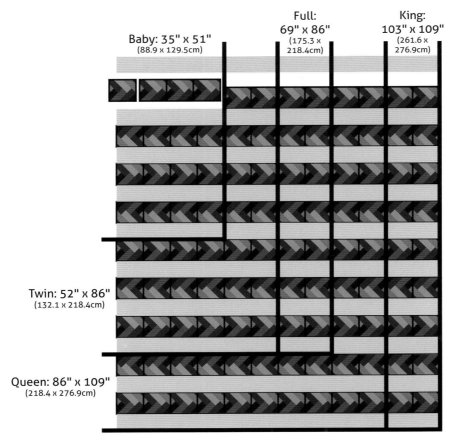

Baby: 35" x 51"
(88.9 x 129.5cm)

Full:
69" x 86"
(175.3 x 218.4cm)

King:
103" x 109"
(261.6 x 276.9cm)

Twin: 52" x 86"
(132.1 x 218.4cm)

Queen: 86" x 109"
(218.4 x 276.9cm)

Quilt layout. Use the number of blocks indicated by the illustration and the chart to construct your quilt to size.

	Baby	Twin	Full	Queen	King
Finished size	35" x 51" (88.9 x 129.5cm)	52" x 86" (132.1 x 218.4cm)	69" x 86" (175.3 x 218.4cm)	86" x 109" (218.4 x 276.9cm)	103" x 109" (261.6 x 276.9cm)
Block configuration	4 rows of 4 block long strips	7 rows of 6 block long strips	7 rows of 8 block long strips	9 rows of 10 block long strips	9 rows of 12 block long strips
Sashing	5 strips of 5" (12.7cm) sashing	8 strips of 5" (12.7cm) sashing	8 strips of 5" (12.7cm) sashing	10 strips of 5" (12.7cm) sashing	10 strips of 5" (12.7cm) sashing
Materials Needed					
Various coordinating prints in at least 5 different fabrics, totaling:	2½ yd. (2.3m)	5½ yd. (5m)	7¼ yd. (6.7m)	11⅓ yd. (10.4m)	13½ yd. (12.4m)
Sashing	1 yd. (1m)	1¾ yd. (1.7m)	2⅓ yds. (2.2m)	3⅔ yd. (3.4m)	4⅓ yd. (3.9m)
Batting	43" x 59" (109.2 x 149.9cm)	60" x 94" (152.4 x 238.8cm)	77" x 94" (195.6 x 238.8cm)	94" x 117" (238.8 x 297.2cm)	111" x 117" (281.9 x 297.2cm)
Backing	1¾ yd. (1.6m) of 60" (152.4cm)-wide backing	1¾ yd. (1.7m) of 106" (269.2cm)-wide backing	2¼ yd. (2.1m) of 106" (269.2cm)-wide backing	2⅔ yd. (2.5m) of 118" (299.7cm)-wide backing	3¼ yd. (3m) of 118" (299.7cm)-wide backing
Binding	½ yd. (0.5m)	⅔ yd. (0.6m)	¾ yd. (0.7m)	1 yd. (1m)	1 yd. (1m)
Coordinating prints					
Strips to cut:	12 strips: 7" (17.8cm) x width of fabric	28 strips: 7" (17.8cm) x width of fabric	37 strips: 7" (17.8cm) x width of fabric	58 strips: 7" (17.8cm) x width of fabric	69 strips: 7" (17.8cm) x width of fabric
Subcut into:	112 rectangles: 4" x 7" (10.2 x 17.8cm)	280 rectangles: 4" x 7" (10.2 x 17.8cm)	364 rectangles: 4" x 7" (10.2 x 17.8cm)	576 rectangles: 4" x 7" (10.2 x 17.8cm)	684 rectangles: 4" x 7" (10.2 x 17.8cm)
Sashing fabric					
Strips to cut:	5 strips: 5½" (14cm) x width of fabric	11 strips: 5½" (14cm) x width of fabric	15 strips: 5½" (14cm) x width of fabric	23 strips: 5½" (14cm) x width of fabric	28 strips: 5½" (14cm) x width of fabric
Prep:	Trim to 35" (88.9cm) strips	Chain all strips, then subcut into 8 strips: 5½" x 52" (14 x 132.1cm)	Chain all strips, then subcut into 8 strips: 5½" x 69" (14 x 175.3cm)	Chain all strips, then subcut into 10 strips: 5½" x 86" (14 x 218.4cm)	Chain all strips, then subcut into 10 strips: 5½" x 103" (14 x 261.6cm)

PRECUT PERFECT!

I found that a collection of fat eighths works nicely for this project. Simply cut 4" (10.2cm)-wide pieces off the 9" (23cm) side of a fat eighth for pieces that are more than big enough to fit the paper piecing pattern. The result will be beautifully coordinated. For the full-size quilts here, you'll need the following number of fat eighths: 28 (baby), 70 (twin), 91 (full), 144 (queen), and 171 (king).

CHAIN BLOCK PURSE QUILT

Use the following chart to cut the pieces and assemble the blocks to form your quilt top. Then refer to the basic quilting guide on page 64 for the steps needed to finish. The quilt is made of rows of the chain block, separated by sashing strips, with every other row flipped to achieve the brick tiling pattern. Note that the size of the blocks has been increased to make creating the quilt top faster and easier, but the assembly is exactly the same.

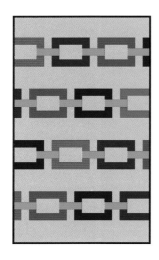

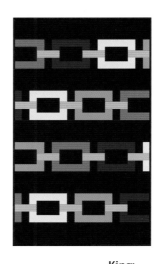

Color variations. Would you like to make this quilt in a different color palette? Check out the options here to spark your creativity.

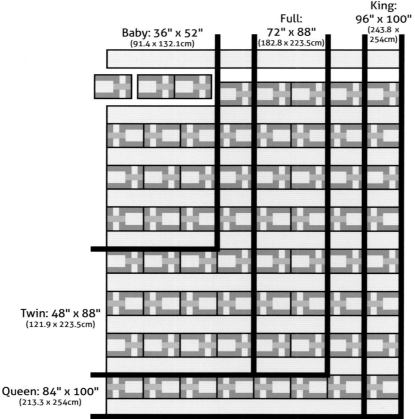

Baby: 36" x 52"
(91.4 x 132.1cm)

Full: 72" x 88"
(182.8 x 223.5cm)

King: 96" x 100"
(243.8 x 254cm)

Twin: 48" x 88"
(121.9 x 223.5cm)

Queen: 84" x 100"
(213.3 x 254cm)

Quilt layout. Use the number of blocks indicated by the illustration and the chart to construct your quilt to size.

	Baby	Twin	Full	Queen	King
Finished size	36" x 52" (91.4 x 132cm)	48" x 88" (121.9 x 223.5cm)	72" x 88" (182.8 x 223.5cm)	84" x 100" (213.3 x 254cm)	96" x 100" (243.8 x 254cm)
Block configuration	3 blocks x 4 blocks (12 total)	4 blocks x 7 blocks (28 total)	6 blocks x 7 blocks (42 total)	7 blocks x 8 blocks (56 total)	8 blocks x 8 blocks (64 total)
Sashing	5 strips of 4" (10.2cm) sashing	8 strips of 4" (10.2cm) sashing	8 strips of 4" (10.2cm) sashing	9 strips of 4" (10.2cm) sashing	9 strips of 4" (10.2cm) sashing
Materials Needed					
Background fabric	1¼ yd. (1.2m)	2½ yd. (2.3m)	3½ yd. (3.2m)	4¾ yd. (4.4m)	5¼ yd. (4.9m)
Chain fabric	¾ yd. (0.7m)	1⅔ yd. (1.6m)	2¼ yd. (2.1m)	3 yd. (2.8m)	3¼ yd. (3m)
Link fabric	¼ yd. (0.3m)	½ yd. (0.5m)	½ yd. (0.5m)	¾ yd. (0.7m)	1 yd. (1m)
Batting	44" x 60" (111.7 x 152.4cm)	56" x 96" (142.2 x 243.8cm)	80" x 96" (203.2 x 243.8cm)	92" x 108" (233.6 x 274.3cm)	104" x 108" (264.1 x 274.3cm)
Backing	1¾ yd. (1.7m) of 60" (152.4cm)-wide backing	1⅔ yd. (1.6m) of 106" (269.2cm)-wide backing	2⅓ yd. (2.2m) of 106" (269.2cm)-wide backing	2⅔ yd. (2.5m) of 118" (299.7cm)-wide backing	3 yd. (2.8m) of 118" (299.7cm)-wide backing
Binding	½ yd. (0.5m)	⅔ yd. (0.6m)	¾ yd. (0.7m)	1 yd. (1m)	1 yd. (1m)
Background fabric					
Strips to cut:	2 strips: 4½" (11.4cm) x width of fabric (A)	5 strips: 4½" (11.4cm) x width of fabric (A)	7 strips: 4½" (11.4cm) x width of fabric (A)	10 strips: 4½" (11.4cm) x width of fabric (A)	11 strips: 4½" (11.4cm) x width of fabric (A)
	3 strips: 2½" (6.4cm) x width of fabric (B)	6 strips: 2½" (6.4cm) x width of fabric (B)	8 strips: 2½" (6.4cm) x width of fabric (B)	11 strips: 2½" (6.4cm) x width of fabric (B)	12 strips: 2½" (6.4cm) x width of fabric (B)
Sashing:	5 strips: 4½" (11.4cm) x width of fabric	11 strips: 4½" (11.4cm) x width of fabric	16 strips: 4½" (11.4cm) x width of fabric	21 strips: 4½" (11.4cm) x width of fabric	23 strips: 4½" (11.4cm) x width of fabric
Prep:	Trim to: 36½" (92.7cm) strips (H)	Chain all strips, then subcut into 8 strips: 4½" x 48½" (11.4 x 123.1cm)	Chain all strips, then subcut into 8 strips: 4½" x 72½" (11.4 x 184.1cm)	Chain all strips, then subcut into 9 strips: 4½" x 84½" (11.4 x 214.6cm)	Chain all strips, then subcut into 9 strips: 4½" x 96½" (11.4 x 245.1cm)
Chain fabric					
Strips to cut:	10 strips: 2½" (6.4cm) x width of fabric (C)	22 strips: 2½" (6.4cm) x width of fabric (C)	30 strips: 2½" (6.4cm) x width of fabric (C)	42 strips: 2½" (6.4cm) x width of fabric (C)	46 strips: 2½" (6.4cm) x width of fabric (C)
Link fabric					
Strips to cut:	2 strips: 2½" (6.4cm) x width of fabric	5 strips: 2½" (6.4cm) x width of fabric	7 strips: 2½" (6.4cm) x width of fabric	10 strips: 2½" (6.4cm) x width of fabric	11 strips: 2½" (6.4cm) x width of fabric
Subcut into:	12 rectangles: 6½" x 2½" (G) (16.5 x 6.4cm)	28 rectangles: 6½" x 2½" (G) (16.5 x 6.4cm)	42 rectangles: 6½" x 2½" (G) (16.5 x 6.4cm)	56 rectangles: 6½" x 2½" (G) (16.5 x 6.4cm)	64 rectangles: 6½" x 2½" (G) (16.5 x 6.4cm)
A/C strip set					
Subcut into:	12 rectangles: 8½" x 6½" (E) (21.6 x 16.5cm)	28 rectangles: 8½" x 6½" (E) (21.6 x 16.5cm)	42 rectangles: 8½" x 6½" (E) (21.6 x 16.5cm)	56 rectangles: 8½" x 6½" (E) (21.6 x 16.5cm)	64 rectangles: 8½" x 6½" (E) (21.6 x 16.5cm)
B/C wide strip set					
Subcut into:	24 rectangles: 6½" x 3½" (F) (16.5 x 8.9cm)	56 rectangles: 6½" x 3½" (F) (16.5 x 8.9cm)	84 rectangles: 6½" x 3½" (F) (16.5 x 8.9cm)	112 rectangles: 6½" x 3½" (F) (16.5 x 8.9cm)	128 rectangles: 6½" x 3½" (F) (16.5 x 8.9cm)

OFFSET SQUARES PANEL CURTAIN QUILT

Use the following chart to cut the pieces and assemble the blocks to form your quilt top. Then refer to the basic quilting guide on page 64 for the steps needed to finish. You'll see that the block layout has been tweaked just a bit to make it more consistent, but the construction is very much the same as described for the curtain.

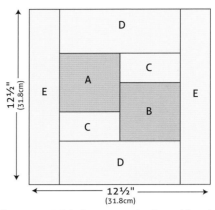

Block layout. Add these vertical and horizontal sashing strips to the offset square units to create a consistent 12½" x 12½" (32 x 32cm) block.

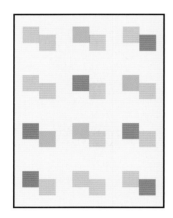
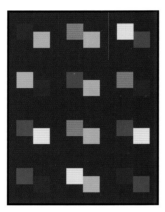
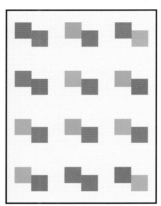

Color variations. Would you like to make this quilt in a different color palette? Check out the options here to spark your creativity.

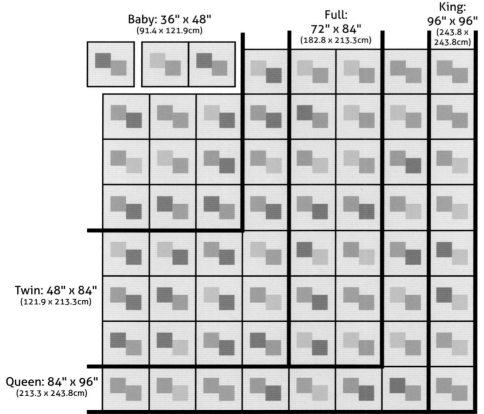

Baby: 36" x 48"
(91.4 x 121.9cm)

Full:
72" x 84"
(182.8 x 213.3cm)

King:
96" x 96"
(243.8 x 243.8cm)

Twin: 48" x 84"
(121.9 x 213.3cm)

Queen: 84" x 96"
(213.3 x 243.8cm)

Quilt layout. Use the number of blocks indicated by the illustration and the chart to construct your quilt to size.

	Baby	Twin	Full	Queen	King
Finished size	36 x 48" (91.4 x 121.9cm)	48" x 84" (121.9 x 213.3cm)	72" x 84" (182.8 x 213.3cm)	84" x 96" (213.3 x 243.8cm)	96" x 96" (243.8 x 243.8cm)
Block configuration	3 blocks x 4 blocks (12 total)	4 blocks x 7 blocks (28 total)	6 blocks x 7 blocks (42 total)	7 blocks x 8 blocks (56 total)	8 blocks x 8 blocks (64 total)
Materials Needed					
Various coordinating focus fabrics, totalling:	½ yd. (0.5m)	1 yd. (1m)	1½ yd. (1.4m)	2 yd. (1.8m)	2¼ yd. (2m)
Background fabrics	1½ yd. (1.4m)	3⅓ yd. (3.1m)	4⅔ yd. (4.3m)	6¼ yd. (5.8m)	7 yd. (6.4m)
Batting	44" x 56" (111.7 x 142.2cm)	56" x 92" (142.2 x 233.6cm)	80" x 92" (203.2 x 233.6cm)	92" x 104" (233.6 x 264.1cm)	104" x 104" (264.1 x 264.1cm)
Backing	1⅓ yd. (1.3m) of 60" (152.4cm)-wide backing	2⅔ yd. (2.5m) of 60" (152.4cm)-wide backing	2⅓ yd. (2.2m) of 106" (269.2cm)-wide backing	2⅔ yd. (2.5m) of 118" (299.7cm)-wide backing	3 yd. (2.8m) of 118" (299.7cm)-wide backing
Binding	½ yd. (0.5m)	⅔ yd. (0.6m)	¾ yd. (0.7m)	1 yd. (1m)	1 yd. (1m)
Coordinating focus fabrics					
Strips to cut:	3 strips: 4½" (11.4cm) x width of fabric	7 strips: 4½" (11.4cm) x width of fabric	11 strips: 4½" (11.4cm) x width of fabric	14 strips: 4½" (11.4cm) x width of fabric	16 strips: 4½" (11.4cm) x width of fabric
Subcut into:	24 squares: 4½ x 4½" (A/B) (11.4 x 11.4cm)	56 squares: 4½ x 4½" (A/B) (11.4 x 11.4cm)	84 squares: 4½ x 4½" (A/B) (11.4 x 11.4cm)	112 squares: 4½ x 4½" (A/B) (11.4 x 11.4cm)	128 squares: 4½ x 4½" (A/B) (11.4 x 11.4cm)
Background prints					
Strips to cut:	11 strips: 2½" (6.4cm) x width of fabric	26 strips: 2½" (6.4cm) x width of fabric	39 strips: 2½" (6.4cm) x width of fabric	52 strips: 2½" (6.4cm) x width of fabric	59 strips: 2½" (6.4cm) x width of fabric
Subcut into:	24 rectangles: 4½" x 2½" (C) (11.4 x 6.4cm)	56 rectangles: 4½" x 2½" (C) (11.4 x 6.4cm)	84 rectangles: 4½" x 2½" (C) (11.4 x 6.4cm)	112 rectangles: 4½" x 2½" (C) (11.4 x 6.4cm)	128 rectangles: 4½" x 2½" (C) (11.4 x 6.4cm)
	24 rectangles: 12½" x 2½" (E) (31.8 x 6.4cm)	56 rectangles: 12½" x 2½" (E) (31.8 x 6.4cm)	84 rectangles: 12½" x 2½" (E) (31.8 x 6.4cm)	112 rectangles: 12½" x 2½" (E) (31.8 x 6.4cm)	128 rectangles: 12½" x 2½" (E) (31.8 x 6.4cm)
Strips to cut:	3 strips: 8½" (21.6cm) x width of fabric	6 strips: 8½" (21.6cm) x width of fabric	8 strips: 8½" (21.6cm) x width of fabric	11 strips: 8½" (21.6cm) x width of fabric	12 strips: 8½" (21.6cm) x width of fabric
Subcut into:	24 rectangles: 8½" x 3½" (D) (21.6 x 8.9cm)	56 rectangles: 8½" x 3½" (D) (21.6 x 8.9cm)	84 rectangles: 8½" x 3½" (D) (21.6 x 8.9cm)	112 rectangles: 8½" x 3½" (D) (21.6 x 8.9cm)	128 rectangles: 8½" x 3½" (D) (21.6 x 8.9cm)

PRECUT PERFECT!

A 5" (12.7cm) charm pack would work perfectly to replace the focus fabrics in this project, ensuring each square is nice and random! Each charm square easily replaces the 4½" (11.5cm) focus square you need. The result will be beautifully coordinated. For the full-size quilts here, you'll need the following number of charm squares: 24 (baby), 56 (twin), 84 (full), 112 (queen), and 128 (king).

BASKET WEAVE POTHOLDER QUILT

Use the following chart to cut the pieces and assemble the blocks to form your quilt top. Then refer to the basic quilting guide on page 64 for the steps needed to finish. Note that to make assembling a full quilt top faster and easier, I've adjusted the blocks to more than double the size of the potholder. The assembly is still the same, but the pieces you are working with will be larger.

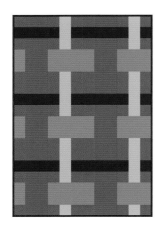

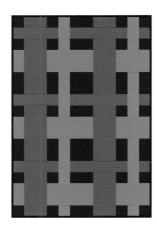

Color variations. Would you like to make this quilt in a different color palette? Check out the options here to spark your creativity.

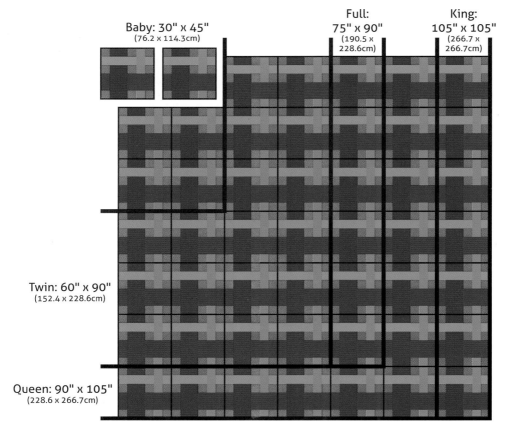

Baby: 30" x 45"
(76.2 x 114.3cm)

Full:
75" x 90"
(190.5 x 228.6cm)

King:
105" x 105"
(266.7 x 266.7cm)

Twin: 60" x 90"
(152.4 x 228.6cm)

Queen: 90" x 105"
(228.6 x 266.7cm)

Quilt layout. Use the number of blocks indicated by the illustration and the chart to construct your quilt to size.